D1026775

HQ 751 .I43

Ingle, Dwight Joyce, 1907-
Who should have children? An
environmental and genetic approach

WHO SHOULD HAVE CHILDREN?

*An Environmental and
Genetic Approach*

DWIGHT J. INGLE

The Bobbs-Merrill Company, Inc.
Publishers

INDIANAPOLIS   NEW YORK

HQ
751
.I43

Copyright © 1973 by The Bobbs-Merrill Company, Inc.
Printed in the United States of America
FIRST PRINTING

Library of Congress Cataloging in Publication Data
  Ingle, Dwight Joyce, 1907–
  Who should have children?
  Bibliography: p.
   1. Eugenics. 2. United States—Population.
3. United States—Social condition—1960–
I. Title. [DNLM: 1. Eugenics. 2. Population
control. 3. Population growth. HQ 751 151w 1973]
HQ751.I43   301.32′1′0973   72–12535
ISBN 0–672–53595–5
ISBN 0–672–63595–X (pbk)

Contents

Preface

"The right of society to continue to exist and to become increasingly free of genetic and environmental handicaps seems more important than the right of an individual to act against the welfare of children and society." At face value, few would likely disagree with Dwight Ingle's position and most would likely embrace it as a legitimate societal aim. However, it is just as likely that many who support this position will not concur with his suggestions for achieving the desired goal.

In direct but nonprofessorial fashion, Dr. Ingle considers hereditary and socio-environmental contributions to the human population and to its manifestations for good and not-so-good. This portion of the book is basically factual and unquestionable. His interpretation of this body of factual knowledge and of its implications for the present and particularly the future of humanity, however, is in a different vein. It is provocative and challenging, thoughtful and persuasive. The fundamental questions he asks are as timely and critical as his answers are achievable and controversial.

This is a personal book, one in which the author declares his position in a positive but sympathetic way. Unfortunately, as Dr. Ingle clearly notes, alternatives for achieving the genetic and social competence of the human population are few. The tough choices are our own and doubtless must be made soon.

EDWARD J. KORMONDY
Olympia, Washington

Acknowledgments

The manuscript of this book has been read by Frank Goodrich, Arthur R. Jensen, Daniel G. Freedman, Victor A. McKusick, Jane Ohly, David Ingle, and Geneva Ingle. I am grateful to each of them for criticisms, corrections, and suggestions. Edward J. Kormondy has edited skillfully, gently, and wisely. Jane Gilpin typed the manuscript carefully and efficiently.

Foreword

Most agencies of government and society and many individuals are concerned about the great social problems of our country and of the world. It is often thought and believed that all causes of social problems are environmental. I believe that in addition to environmental causes there are genetic (hereditary) causes of some of the social problems of mankind. Environmental and genetic causes interact and reinforce one another, so I shall discuss both.

I have been interested in the problems of man most of my life. As a boy on the farm I saw many people who needed help from others. There was a great deal of poverty. Many children died in infancy or in early life. The hungry, the sick, the mentally ill, and the mentally retarded received little help other than that given by members of the family or by good neighbors. When I went away to school, I saw the slums of our great cities and lived through the Depression of the thirties. I first worked with the mentally ill and the mentally retarded and then turned my attention to experimental medicine and the causes of some diseases. I have been close to the problems of health, competence, and welfare most of my life.

Fashions in belief about the importance of heredity and environment in human affairs have gone through cycles. I had some professors who believed that environment is all-important, but other professors were equally certain that heredity alone determines the destiny of each of us. I became convinced that none of them really knew and each was merely repeating the dogma that he had been taught. The debate is an old one. For example, several generations ago Alfred Lord Tennyson wrote:

> Envy wears the mask of love,
> And, laughing sober fact to scorn,
> Cries to weakest as to strongest,
> "Ye are equals, equal-born."
> Equal-born? O yes,
> If yonder hill be level with the flat.
> Charm us, orator,
> Till the lion look no larger than the cat.

Historically, the idea that heredity is of major importance in determining the nature of man has been used to support the inheriting of wealth, power, and special privileges and the placing of leadership in the hands of a few families. Belief in biological equality at birth has been used to justify the more communistic forms of government. When scientific questions become political, people become emotional about them and it is difficult to debate and study them.

The crimes of the German Fascists in putting to death the "biologically unfit" and in trying to exterminate the Jews, whom they called "inferior," so horrified mankind that many people choose to accept the dogma that heredity is not important in human affairs. The crimes of Hitler were not based on scientific knowledge about heredity.

Attempts to solve our social problems are usually based on two general assumptions: first, that all the causes of our social problems are environmental, and second, that these problems can be solved by spending large amounts of money. None of our major aims has been achieved. Some problems, such as crime and drug abuse, steadily worsen. The number of people on welfare continues to rise. Increased spending for health care has not reduced our overall health problems during the past ten years. We are pouring increasing amounts of money into education, but the average achievements of children in our schools have not increased. The population explosion ranks next to war itself as a threat to our future.

I believe that some of our social problems having to do with health, education, and job success have biological as well as environmental causes that could be reduced by selective population control. By this I mean that millions of people are unqualified for parenthood and should remain childless. This is a controversial idea. I present my arguments for it in this book.

DWIGHT J. INGLE
Chicago, November, 1972

I

Some General Considerations

AIM

This book is written to justify selective population control. Overpopulation is a grave threat to the future of man; some forms of control are needed if we are to avoid famine, disease, and war as checks on population growth. I believe that man must limit his numbers and that therefore efforts to control births should be focused on those who for cultural, genetic, or medical reasons are unable to endow children with a reasonable chance to achieve health, happiness, self-sufficiency, and good citizenship. I believe that health institutions and agencies should be concerned with selective birth control as a part of preventive and community medicine and as a means of reducing social problems. I believe that selective population control is a practical, humane alternative to a growing welfare state. I believe in the right of society to exercise intelligent control over its future rather than to submit passively to irresponsible threats to its welfare and dignity. I will discuss the ethics of these recommendations as well as the reasons for them.

There are two general aims among those who would try to control the biology of man. The first is to try to produce supermen. I am opposed to this aim. The second is to reduce the causes of incompetence and poor health without otherwise reducing genetic differences among individuals. I favor this aim. Differences in race, physique, intellect, abilities, interests, etc., should not be destroyed, for they add to the richness of human life. Any program of selective population control should be free from government direction; it should retain freedom of choice. Such a program should accompany, not replace, programs to improve the environment of man and to ensure equal rights and opportunities.

INDIVIDUALITY

Every human being is unique; each person differs from every other. The most simple way of showing that this is true is to compare fingerprints. When careful studies are made of physical, biochemical, and psychological characteristics, it may be shown that even so-called "identical" twins differ at least slightly and sometimes significantly. The same seems to be true of everything that lives. We may find marked similarity but not complete identity.

Human equality is not the same as human identity. Although each of us is biologically and psychologically unique, we should have equal rights to opportunities for self-fulfillment and for achieving human dignity, and equal rights before the law. We should not judge human beings to be "superior" or "inferior" in respect to human worth on the basis of biological differences. Man has used the words "superior" and "inferior" too carelessly and has got into a great deal of unnecessary trouble because of it.

It is much more exciting to be unique than to be identical with others. Think of some differences that are easily observed. Adults range in size from dwarfs to circus giants. Strength ranges from helplessness in some sick people to the ability of a few strong men to lift more than two tons from the floor when in a harness. Others can run 100 yards in 9.1 seconds. A few can jump over a bar 7 feet high. Athletes differ widely in the kinds of physical feats they do best. Intelligence ranges from that of the idiot to that of the genius. An individual who excels in some form of creativity may behave stupidly when shopping for groceries or when trying to keep a household account; his or her political beliefs may also be foolish. Body forms vary from those which rival Venus or Apollo to the hideously deformed bodies commonly hidden behind closed doors. All kinds of people make up the world. Much of this diversity is good, but some of it represents human misery and should be avoided if man can learn how to do it.

COMPLEXITY OF CAUSES

Most human problems are an outcome of many causes. This may be said of most events in nature. Anyone who has experience raising plants knows that both seed and soil are important. Water is also vital. The importance of light in the health and growth of plants is easily shown by putting them in the dark. We find when soil is carefully studied that certain compounds, trace elements, and bacteria are needed for normal plant growth. Temperature is also a factor. The causes that affect the reproduction, growth, and health of animals are just as numerous. Almost any natural process is affected by many factors. I mention this because man has a tendency to look for a single cause of each problem; even scientists make this mistake. It is not the way things are.

In addition to recognizing that a number of factors are involved in causing each human problem, we must also realize that it is possible to reach the same final result by different means. The old saying, "There is more than one way to skin a cat," illustrates the principle that is sometimes given the fancy name "equifinality." It is generally possible to arrive at the same destination by any one of several routes. You may make a man angry, sad, or happy by any one of numerous means. A man may be made sick by a blow on the head, exposure to heat or cold, an infection, a bone fracture, almost any kind of a severe stress, or sometimes by the loss of a loved one. I cannot think of any important human problem that has a single cause.

REQUIREMENTS FOR PROOF

When a scientist tries to explain a process, a thing, or a happening, his hypothesis should be reasonable and should account for all the facts. The evidence must be confirmed by other scientists; beware those who claim that they alone can make correct observations or carry out the right experiments. All other reasonable explanations should be ruled out. The explanation should permit prediction and control of the kind of happening under study. For example, before concluding that environment alone determines the level of intelligence, it should be possible to make dull children into bright children by manipulation of the environment. Finally, the explanation should be acceptable to most of the scientists interested in the problem. Sometimes scientists do not agree and then it is necessary to have more research and debate.

FALLACIES IN REASONING

Most of us make mistakes in reasoning about causes and effects. These errors in reasoning are called *fallacies.* One of the best known is *post hoc, ergo propter hoc* reasoning; the meaning of this Latin phrase is "after this, therefore because of this." When one kind of event is followed regularly by another kind of event, it is easy to imagine that the first caused the second. Sometimes this is true, but sometimes it is not. The crowing of roosters before the dawn does not cause the sunrise. It is commonly believed by both physicians and patients that when a patient gets well after receiving a medicine that the medicine caused the improvement. Sometimes this is true. But some diseases improve without treatment. This is what a doctor means when he says that a disease is self-limiting. The common cold goes away whether medicine is given or not. In order to avoid giving undeserved credit to a new drug that is being tested, a medical scientist may select a number of patients having the disease that the drug is expected to benefit. He divides the patients into two groups, gives the new drug to one group and a dummy preparation (one that looks exactly like the new medicine but is made of inert substances) to the other. This is called a *controlled clinical trial* and the dummy medicine is called a *placebo.* None of the patients knows whether he is receiving the new drug or the placebo. If the medical scientist is really on his toes, he does the study so that the physicians judging the results of therapy are also unaware of which patients are getting the new drug and which the placebo. In this way suggestion and wishful thinking cannot influence either the patients or those who are judging the benefit to the patients. This is called a *double-blind placebo control study*.

A fallacy closely related to *post hoc* reasoning is to assume that there must be a causal connection between correlated events. Correlation means that two or more sets of values rise or fall together. The increase in sales of Volkswagens, for instance, has accompanied the increase in cases of lung cancer, but there is no direct causal connection. There is, however, a direct causal relationship between the number of cars being driven and the amount of air pollution.

When we study any kind of population—whether rocks, plants, mice, or human beings—it is almost never possible to study all the individuals that make up the population. It is necessary to select a sample of individuals that represents the population under study. After studying a representative sample, we may then generalize from the data collected on the sample to the population from which the sample was drawn. This is called *inductive* reasoning; it is basic to most scientific research and reasoning but it too may lead to errors. The sample may be too small; it may not be properly selected. A sample is said to be "biased" when it does not properly represent the entire group. Suppose that a physician studying arthritis selected only athletes as subjects; this would be an example of an error in sampling.

Another common fallacy in reasoning is to overgeneralize. Statements that all poor people are lazy or that all unemployed people want to work are examples of overgeneralization. When a doctor prescribes penicillin for every patient who has a cold, he is also overgeneralizing. We sometimes make unfair generalizations about racial and national groups. Racial and national identity are of no value in predicting the social worth of individuals. There are wide individual differences among the people making up any large group. If somebody tells you that "blondes have more fun," this is an example of the fallacy of overgeneralization.

What I have said about research methods, requirements for proof, and errors in research and reasoning is intended to show that it is difficult to study complex problems and to learn the causes of problems. Science does have a large body of knowledge that is generally accepted, but the search for new knowledge keeps the scientist thinking and saying "Maybe" and "Probably so." It is important for each individual to remain free to disagree with his fellows and to ask for better evidence on any subject that is important in human affairs. I ask the reader to remember this if he finds me becoming too dogmatic in the pages that follow.

I have a retired medical scientist friend, Dr. Carl A. Dragstedt, who writes humorous verse. He expressed the gist of what I have said as follows:

> So don't be too hasty
> At drawing conclusions,
> For nature has furnished
> Many confusions.

Scientists may also disagree about statistics. I shall often give figures on the numbers of people represented in social problems and on the costs of these problems and of the efforts to correct them. Most of these figures are rough estimates. Even when precise figures are known, they change as time goes by; some changes will occur between the time of writing this book and the time of publication. So do not be surprised if you find someone else giving somewhat different figures. Moreover, there is overlapping in estimates of costs. For instance, the total cost of education includes the costs of health education and of research. Some of the figures for these costs are also included in estimates of total spending for health. The total cost of education may further include the costs of efforts to reeducate criminals and to educate against crime; the same figures are added into estimates of the total cost of crime. Finally, there is overlap in estimates of the total cost of health care and the total cost of welfare; some of the same expenses get counted in both.

II

The Nature of
Heredity and Environment

Heredity means transmission of certain characteristics from parents to children; the word generally refers to biological traits. The related word "inheritance," however, is sometimes used in a broader sense: we speak of cultural and legal inheritance as well as biological inheritance. In this book I will write about biological (genetic) inheritance and cultural (social) inheritance. I use the word "culture" to mean the ideas, attitudes, and habits that people learn from their families and from social experiences rather than to mean social and intellectual refinement.

Environment means all the conditions, circumstances, and influences other than those that are inborn. There are three classes of environmental effects. The first is biological and includes such things as conditions within the uterus (womb), the food we eat, and the drugs we take. The second is physical, such as the pressure, temperature, and humidity of the air; radiation; light; gravity;

and noise. The third is the social environment, which begins at birth and includes all our experiences with other people in the home, schools, and society.

From the little that I have said you can already see that there is an overlapping of the influences of heredity and environment. We cannot clearly separate their actions and effects because they begin to interact the moment a male sperm cell fertilizes a female egg cell. The factors carried by the sperm cell and egg cell that determine biological heredity are called *genes*. The word "genetic," which I will use frequently, refers to biological inheritance.

HEREDITY

In all higher forms of life, including man, a new life begins when an egg cell from a female is fertilized by a sperm cell from a male. These human cells are very small. If you placed 200 egg cells side by side they would extend about 1 inch. About 5000 sperm cells could be placed side by side in the space of 1 inch. A sperm cell looks rather like a tadpole. It has a round head and a long tail that enables it to swim in the moisture of the vagina, uterus, and fallopian tubes (these connect the ovaries to the uterus, one for each of the two ovaries). The sexually mature woman releases an egg cell from one or the other of her two ovaries about every twenty-eight days. It passes from the ovary into the fallopian tube and moves towards the uterus. If it is entered by a sperm cell—one of millions that are ejaculated during sexual intercourse— the genetic material (genes) of the sperm cell and egg cell are joined together.

It was once believed that biological traits are carried

from parent to child by blood. This was the origin of the expressions "good blood" and "bad blood" and the phrase, "Blood will tell." Hereditary traits are not carried from parent to child by blood but only by sperm and egg cells.

If you were to look at the head of a sperm cell under a microscope, you would see a round body near the center of the cell. This is the nucleus of the cell. When the nucleus is stained with a dye so that parts of it become visible, you can see forty-six rod-shaped bodies inside the nucleus. Actually they are arranged into twenty-three pairs. An equal number of these rods is found inside the nucleus of an egg cell. These individual rods are called "chromosomes," and each is made of thousands of chemical compounds called "genes." Genes are the units of biological heredity. It is estimated that there are about 25,000 genes in a set of human chromosomes.

Each gene is a kind of complex chemical compound called deoxyribonucleic acid, or DNA for short. DNA is made up of more simple compounds, known as purines and pyrimidines or, for our purposes, as nitrogen-bases. The way these nitrogen-bases are arranged in the gene provides an information code guiding the development of a new life. Individual genes are parts of larger DNA chains. It is estimated that there are more than seven million genetic messages coded into the genes, although sometimes a single gene determines an inherited trait. A single gene may also be involved in a number of messages. Sometimes scientists speak of genes as biological blueprints.

When the sperm cell enters the egg cell, the genetic material from each is joined together. When the newly fertilized egg cell begins to divide, each of the two new cells gets forty-six chromosomes with genes that were reproduced from the genes of both the father and the mother. The fertilized egg cell first divides into two cells, then four, eight, sixteen, and so on and presently begins to take shape as a human embryo. All stages of growth and development into a person are controlled by genes.

Soon after the fertilized egg cell begins to divide, it moves on down the fallopian tube into the uterus and attaches itself to the wall of the uterus. It now becomes an embryo that develops a placenta with blood vessels that carry oxygen and food from the mother to the embryo. The embryo develops its own heart and blood vessels, some of which spread through the placenta and allow the exchange of fluid, oxygen, and nutrients between the blood of the embryo and that of the mother. After eight weeks the embryo becomes a fetus. If all goes well, the fetus develops into a baby, which is born about nine months after conception. The placenta is expelled from the uterus soon after the baby is born and is commonly called the *afterbirth*.

Some genes are dominant and others recessive. If an individual inherits a dominant gene from each parent, the trait determined by that gene will be seen in that individual. The same is true when an individual inherits a dominant gene from just one parent. If an individual inherits the same recessive gene from each parent, the corresponding trait will develop. If a recessive gene is inherited from just one parent, the trait does not develop but that recessive gene may be passed on to his or her children.

To make this more specific, let us consider the inheritance of eye color. If an individual inherits genes for brown eyes (dominant) from each parent, then he or she will have brown eyes. If the individual inherits a gene for brown eyes (dominant) from one parent and a gene for blue eyes (recessive) from the other parent, that person will have brown eyes but may pass genes for both brown and blue eyes to his or her children. If the individual inherits a gene for blue eyes from each parent, then his or her eyes will be blue. Two brown-eyed parents each carrying a recessive gene for blue eyes may sometimes produce a blue-eyed child. When both parents pass on genes for both brown and blue eyes, then some children may have brown eyes and others blue, depending on how the genes get combined in each child. The combination of genes differs in each child except when identical twins grow from one fertilized egg cell that divides into two individuals at the very beginning. It is important to remember that ordinary brothers and sisters are not identical in genetic endowment. Sperm cells from the same man may have a number of genes in common —hence family resemblance—but other genes may differ. The same is true of egg cells from the same woman.

Some biological inheritance is just as simple as the case I have described, but other physical and mental traits are affected by several genes rather than one, and this complicates the study of heredity. I have oversimplified this description of heredity in order to provide a general understanding of the subjects to be discussed in this book. (For additional information, read the books by the following authors listed under Suggested Readings at the end of this book: V. A. McKusick, E. P. Volpe, D. E. Keller.)

INBREEDING

The most practical guide to selective breeding is the old principle, "Like begets like." Breeders of plants and animals have used this principle to develop many purebred varieties. Inbreeding—the mating of brothers and sisters or other close relatives—is frequently used to speed up the development of new strains of animals. Inbreeding brings good traits together, but it also brings together harmful recessive traits. This is the biological reason why closely related people are not allowed to marry; genetic defects appear more frequently among inbred plants and animals. In plant and animal inbreeding, the defective individuals are cast aside. Of course it would not be humane to do this with human beings. A great deal of trial and error remains in plant and animal breeding.

ENVIRONMENT

There are a number of categories of environmental influences. Some are easily observed and measured but others are more subtle. For instance, a great deal is known about the food requirements for growth and reproduction in man. Some scientists feel that knowledge in this field is practically complete and that no further research is needed except to develop plentiful supplies of essential foods. But there is more to learn about the relationship of foods to the ability of man to resist infections and the relationship of diet to diseases of the brain, heart, arteries, liver, and to diabetes. Overeating commonly leads to an increase in some diseases and to a shorter-than-average life span. It has been shown that some animals live longer than average when fed smaller than average amounts of food during their lives.

The baby in the uterus is practically free of germs. Following birth, however, it becomes host to many kinds of viruses and bacteria. Some bacteria are beneficial, such as those which play a part in digestion, but others are potentially harmful. The body has a natural immunity to some of them and develops an immunity to others following exposure to them. Other bacteria and viruses do cause diseases that can scar, cripple, and kill. Not much is known of the functions, if any, of the harmless bacteria and viruses that live in human tissues.

Physical factors in the environment such as temperature, humidity, rain, snow, and storms have affected the evolution and migration of peoples as well as their health, customs, and behavior. The amount of radiation—there is always some radiation from radioactive materials on earth, from the sun, and from outer space—affects the number of changes in genes (mutations). Some chemical agents that we eat, drink, breathe, or get on our skin can cause mutations, too. A mutation is a change in a gene, or sometimes it is the loss of a gene. Most mutations are harmful and may cause the organism to have a new disease, a defect, or to die. About 1 percent of mutations are beneficial.

Gravity is another physical factor in the environment, but its pull is constant and it does not ordinarily cause differences among individuals. But man may become confused and upset if he is put into the condition of being weightless. The astronauts who ride rocket ships outside the pull of the Earth's gravity must undergo long periods of training in order to adapt to weightlessness.

Noise and the pollution of air are other physical factors in the environment that can affect man's health and peace of mind.

Man inherits little, if any, knowledge, only some reflexes and perhaps some instincts. Otherwise, knowledge is learned from the environment. Man's brain does inherit an organization of nerve cells which enables him to behave like a human being. Following the rise of civilization, man's progress has been primarily social rather than biological. In theory, all knowledge is available to all men. Learning and training are responsible for most human behavior, attitudes, and customs. If man lived without social experiences, he would have no language; this is his principal tool of thought. He might, if he survived, learn a few things about shelter and food gathering by trial and error. It is unlikely that any isolated individual would progress very far.

Behavioral scientists and psychiatrists know much and guess more about the subtle influences of social experiences on human behavior. Among these influences are the effects of psychic trauma, frustrations, and sexual experiences on wants, attitudes, and drives. It seems likely that such effects are real, but at present this field of medicine is filled with contradictory beliefs and theories.

It does seem clear, however, that individuals learn their attitudes, beliefs, prejudices, and many of their likes and dislikes. Think about the widely differing beliefs represented by religions, political parties, nations, social subgroups, differences in preferences for foods, clothing, customs, and so on. These are clearly environmental in origin.

Many social scientists claim that environment is all-important in determining what becomes of a person and what causes the problems of society. Having reached this conclusion, they refuse to consider the importance of heredity. It is a fallacy to conclude that because one set of factors is important, no other set of factors can be important.

THE INTERACTION OF HEREDITY AND ENVIRONMENT

From the time an egg cell is fertilized by a sperm cell, it is interacting with its environment. The nourishment that comes to it through the blood of the mother is a part of the biological environment and is necessary for the growth, development and organization of cells which are controlled by the genes.

The uterus of most healthy mothers provides an almost perfect environment for the embryo, and each uterus is very much like another. But things can and do go wrong. If the mother is undernourished, the embryo may also be undernourished. If the mother takes addictive drugs, the baby may be born a drug addict. Some chemical agents and medicines taken by the mother during pregnancy and some diseases of the mother during pregnancy—such as German measles—can cause birth defects. Sometimes an imbalance of the mother's hormones affects and even harms the baby. As soon as the baby leaves the sheltered environment of the uterus, it is exposed to new environmental influences such as light, changes in temperature, sounds, bacteria, viruses, and social stimuli. These influences and those of the genes interact in human development.

Some inherited traits are not significantly affected by environment. Eye color is an example. The color of skin is inherited, but it may be darkened by exposure to sunlight and by certain drugs and hormones.

Body size and body form are both inherited and may both be modified significantly by environment. Body growth may be stunted by starvation and by some drugs. There are strains of dwarf animals in several species, including man. This is an inherited defect due to a lack of the growth hormone from the anterior lobe of the pituitary gland. (See Suggested Readings, page 140, for a book in which the subject of hormones is discussed by R. Le-Baron.) In human beings this gland is about the size of a walnut and lies in a bony pocket of the skull at the base of the brain. It is possible to make a young dwarf grow by injecting growth hormone into its body. Increased food intake also affects the growth of dwarf animals in some species, although in the absence of growth hormone most of the food gets turned into fat rather than bone and muscle. Improved nutrition cannot fully correct the growth defect of dwarfs in any species. Young normal animals of several species may be made to show increased skeletal growth as well as obesity by overfeeding them. Each generation of Americans has a greater average height than that of their parents because of improved nutrition. The people of Japan have changed their food habits since World War II, and the young adults are much taller than their parents. Heredity lays down a capacity for growth which environment, and nutrition especially, can modify but not nullify. Thus children of tall people and children of short people all tend to grow taller when nutrition is improved, but the family differences in average height still occur. Body size is clearly determined by the interaction of heredity and environment.

The principle seems to be the same in respect to intelligence. If a baby inherits a defective brain or a tiny brain, it cannot learn more than simple kinds of responses and self-control. No amount of teaching or environmental advantages will make the child normal in his behavior and ability to learn. Similarly, a child who inherits a brain capable of developing in a good environment into that of a genius would not even learn to talk if he were raised in isolation from others. He could not acquire a culture, social behavior, or any of the great stores of knowledge in books and pictures. Intellect is developed by environmental experiences according to the inherited capacity of the nervous system to learn, reason, and create. Life itself and the individuality of all living things represent the interactions of heredity and environment.

III

Health

COSTS

Throughout the world more people are ill and malnourished than are well. In 1970 the World Health Organization of the United Nations estimated that more than two-thirds of the people of the world were existing on a caloric level of under 2000 calories per day. The United States is spending a total of more than 75 billion dollars per year for health purposes. This figure includes the costs of research and medical education. It is estimated by the market-research firm of Frost and Sullivan that the annual cost of health care will reach 200 billion dollars by 1980; more conservative estimates set the figure at 140 billion dollars. Personal medical care expenses exceed 40 billion dollars a year, and our federal government is spending about 15 billion dollars a year on health, hospitals, and sanitation.

LIFE EXPECTANCY

The economic cost of human health care is less important than the price paid in human suffering for inadequate health care. There is no convincing evidence that illness is now being significantly reduced by our expanding health programs. Of course there have been some medical triumphs. The prevention of poliomyelitis is one. There is progress in treating some cancers. An increased number of the mentally ill may be treated effectively by recently developed medicines. Some patients are restored to health by heart surgery. There is also significant progress in the prevention and control of other diseases. All of us will die some day, but most would like to live a normal life span without serious illness. During the past ten years, there has been an increase of about one year in the average length of life of women in the United States. There has been no increase in the average length of life of men. However, the number of old people and the medical problems of old age are increasing. Illnesses caused by the overuse of alcohol and abuse of drugs are increasing. The growing pollution of air, water, and soil is causing new health problems. Many people who need medical care do not receive it. Medical and hospital costs are rising rapidly, and there is a shortage of nurses and doctors.

Now consider the case of members of cults and religions who do not seek medical care when they are sick. What is the life expectancy of these people as compared to the average for all people who die in the United States? *It is only about a year less than average.* Does this mean that modern medicine has done no more than add a year to the average span of life? No; the figure is misleading. Medical science has more than doubled life expectancy in the past 200 years. It has done this by such preventive measures as sanitation, improved nutrition, water purification, vaccination, health education, and other public health measures. Those who refuse to go to doctors benefit from preventive medicine as much as anyone. Even if they do not become vaccinated, general programs of vaccination prevent epidemics from getting started and everyone becomes protected. Another factor is that many of the people who rely on faith healing have better than average health habits and usually live away from slums.

It is true, however, that going to a physician after a serious disease develops does not affect life span as much as is commonly supposed. Doctors may bring relief from suffering independently of an effect on length of life. There is a saying among doctors: "Medicine sometimes cures, frequently benefits, and always consoles."

There is another important fact that is little known, even among physicians. We talk about cancer and heart disease as our greatest medical problems. There is another class of diseases that causes an even greater loss of "life years." I refer to birth defects. There are many different sorts of defects and many different causes, some of them genetic. About one in every sixteen children is born with a defect. Many of these children die in early life thereby losing many more years from normal life expectancy than do patients who die at older ages of cancer and heart disease. So birth defects represent a great medical problem. (See Suggested Readings, page 140, for E. P. Volpe's book on this subject.)

THE ROLE OF ENVIRONMENT

You probably know and understand the general environmental factors that influence health and length of life. A great deal is published about them in magazines and newspapers and much is said of them on radio and television. I shall review them briefly.

Starvation, germs, parasites, and viruses cause the greatest amount of human sickness throughout the world. In America there is still an abundance of food and relatively few people die of starvation. Some are undernourished because of poverty, some eat harmful substances, a larger number do not select a balanced diet, and a large number eat too much.

In America, public health measures have greatly reduced deaths from bacterial diseases by quarantine, sanitation, control of carriers of disease such as rats and lice, and by the use of antibiotics. But bacteria can develop strains which are resistant to antibiotics, and germ-carrying insects can develop strains which are resistant to insecticides. There is a continuing need to develop new antibiotics and insecticides that will control new strains resistant to the old ones. The battle against them never stops, and medical scientists fear that some insects, germs and viruses will get out of control and cause great epidemics.

This is a good time to mention that bacteria and viruses have genes just as have all forms of life. Many of the basic advances in genetics have come from studying forms of life that are very small. A virus is much smaller than a germ or cell. It cannot reproduce by itself and has to enter a living cell to do so. Sometimes a portion of the genetic information of a virus gets incorporated into that of the cell and causes it to behave abnormally. Viruses can multiply very rapidly within the cell; some cause diseases and some are harmless. A mutation in a harmless germ or virus sometimes makes it harmful; in other words, a new disease may begin from a mutation.

Mutations may also start new strains of germs that are resistant to antibiotics. (Remember that a mutation is a change in a gene or the dropping out of a gene; this genetic change is transmitted to offspring.)

We hear and read a great deal about the harmful effects of mercury, lead, pesticides, and detergents in the soil and water. There are sometimes harmful compounds in the air we breathe. It is not easy to study the long-term effects of air pollution on the health of man. Suppose that a medical scientist finds the incidence of disease is higher than average in the most polluted areas of great cities. Association, however, does not prove cause-and-effect relationships. When an area is frequently polluted, people who can afford to move to cleaner air are likely to do so. They leave behind the poor who cannot afford to move away. Many of the poor have substandard nutrition, sanitation, health education, and medical care. Moreover, some of them may have become poor because of ill health. Any or all of these factors may cause the higher-than-average amount of disease in the area. Medical scientists cannot select a representative sample of people, divide them into "clean air" and "polluted air" groups, keep all other factors the same, and then say to all these people, "You must live where you are for ten or twenty years in order for us to determine whether dirty air makes people sick." Medical research is difficult. The medical scientist does the best he can studying people who move around a lot in a changing environment. If he finds that the number of hospital admissions and deaths rises on days when air pollution is high and falls when the pollution is low, this is evidence for acute effects of air pollution on public health. He may do carefully controlled studies of the effects of polluted air and water on laboratory animals, but the results of animal experimentation do not always apply to man. One factor is that most animals have a much shorter span of life than does the average human being.

There are also psychological and social factors in the environment, some acting directly and some indirectly, that cause disease. Prolonged exposure to loud sounds may harm the inner ear and cause nervous tensions and illnesses. The battle with traffic, crowding, pressures to advance socially and financially, family and social conflicts are all thought to lead to psychological ills and neuroses and to such diseases as high blood pressure and ulcers. Psychoanalysts believe that some psychological causes of disease are very subtle and may be based on experiences that we cannot recall. Alcohol and drug abuse are closely linked with psychological stresses, and they interact with them to cause major health problems.

THE ROLE OF HEREDITY

It has been estimated that heredity plays a major role in as many as 1500 diseases. No one knows exactly how many, but it seems safe to generalize and say that heredity plays a major or a moderate or a minor role in almost all diseases. There are some exceptions. An accidental injury may leave any person crippled and ill. Any person may be made ill by an insufficiency of protein or any number of essential food factors such as vitamins and minerals.

How do living organisms get defective genes in the first place? As I have said before, they arise as mutations. This means that something happened to the gene to knock out a bit of its information code or to change it. An entire gene may be lost or made inactive. This creates an error in the genetic information that controls growth and functions. A mutation may be caused by chemicals and by viral agents. Exposure to X rays or other kinds of radiation will do it. Several years ago, much was said about the danger to genes from radioactive particles blown as dust around the world after the testing of nuclear weapons. There is some natural radioactivity around us all the time. Sometimes a radioactive particle too tiny to see or feel hits a gene and changes it. This has been going on since life began on Earth.

Mutations are an important means to biological changes, both good and bad. Most mutations are harmful, but about 1 percent are beneficial. The harmful mutations frequently lead to the death of the organism, most of them before birth, and thereby drop out without being passed on to new generations. This selective survival of beneficial mutations and the dropping out of harmful mutations explains how mutations can lead to evolution even when most of them are harmful. Harmful mutations may cause genetic defects. Today, medical scientists may keep alive many individuals bearing genetic defects so that the harmful genes which cause defects may be passed on to new generations.

There is another general class of genetic defects. Each cell nucleus contains chromosomes which are made up of genes. The chromosomes may be broken or damaged in the process of cell division, by X rays and other kinds of radiation, or by certain chemicals. They sometimes heal but not always in the right way; the wrong parts may grow together. Sometimes there is an extra chromosome or one may be lost. These defects may cause diseases that are inherited. An embryo bearing a chromosomal defect is much more likely to die in the uterus than is an embryo with normal chromosomes. This is a larger kind of genetic defect than a change in one of the genes within a chromosome. It is possible to see abnormal chromosomes under a microscope.

Earlier I noted that individual sperm cells from the same male are not identical with respect to the genes in them. The same is true of egg cells. One child of a family might inherit a defect—dwarfism for example—but have normal brothers and sisters. Another might carry and pass on a defective recessive gene without developing the defect; brothers and sisters might not carry the defective gene. When an individual inherits the same defective recessive gene from each parent, then he or she will develop the defect or disease. Heredity is complicated, and trying to predict just what traits and diseases will be transmitted from parents to children is risky. There are many facts about the inheritance of diseases that are not mentioned in this book. (Books by McKusick and Volpe listed in Suggested Readings give more information.)

The development of some diseases is determined solely by heredity. Other diseases, such as tuberculosis, are caused primarily by certain germs but have a genetic basis for a person's susceptibility or resistance to those germs. The heredity of germs is important, too. Some strains of the same kind of germs are deadly and other strains are weak. The resistance of the individual to infection is influenced by factors such as prior exposure to germs, age, nutrition, and maybe air pollution. Even psychological factors are said to affect resistance to the tubercle bacillus (the kind of germ that causes tuberculosis) as well as the course of the disease after it develops.

There are hundreds of diseases caused by single defective genes. Most of these—sickle-cell anemia being an exception—are rare. Some genetic defects, such as colorblindness, are not a sickness. Others do cause serious diseases—hemophilia (being a "bleeder"), muscular dystrophy, Huntington's chorea, cystic fibrosis of the pancreas, cystic diseases of the kidney, and many others.

The selective breeding of laboratory animals has produced strains that develop diabetes, high blood pressure, cancers, some diseases of nerves and muscles, and ulcers. Other strains have been developed by selective breeding that are resistant to these diseases. There are also strain differences in resistance to infection. There is good evidence that genes play an important role in causing most of the great diseases of man such as cancers, gout, diseases of the heart and blood vessels, diabetes, and several mental diseases. Most of the great killing diseases are affected by many factors that have not been fully identified. Some people live all of their lives without getting any of the ordinary infectious diseases—even when exposed to them —or cancer, cardiovascular diseases, mental diseases, or any of the so-called "degenerative" diseases. They grow old gracefully and remain active until they quietly fail and die. There seems to be a genetic basis for such good fortune. Doctors have been telling us for a long time, "If you want to be healthy and live a long life, choose your parents carefully."

I have mentioned that sickle-cell anemia is an exception to the general rule that most of the diseases caused by a single defective gene are rare. In this disease there are too few red blood cells and those that are present tend to be long and curved, something like a crescent or sickle. For some reason it occurs far more frequently among Negroes than in people of other races. It is caused by a recessive gene and must be inherited from both the father and mother before the disease develops to its fullest extent. When this gene is inherited from just one parent, there is a small amount of sickling. Carriers of the recessive gene for sickle-cell anemia tend to have a much higher than usual resistance to infection by malaria; this protection has been important to the survival of African Negroes. This claim is commonly accepted but is also disputed.

High blood pressure seems to run in families. It seems probable that inheritance of the tendency to develop this disease involves several genes. This is called *polygenic inheritance* ("poly" means several). Other biological factors in the environment such as smoking, the amounts and kinds of fat in food, and the amount or lack of exercise affect that level of blood pressure and the risk of heart attacks and stroke. The amount of ordinary table salt in the diet affects the blood pressure of some individuals.

Most of the great diseases are apparently caused by a number of genetic and environmental factors which interact.

THE FUTURE

It is sometimes said that the medical profession is working to put itself out of business. Is it reasonable to hope that medical science can eliminate all diseases? Not really. Even if it were possible to rid mankind of all the environmental and genetic causes of diseases, we would still need doctors to care for the mother and baby, to treat victims of accidents, and to care for the aged. The nearly complete elimination of smallpox, diphtheria, scarlet fever, poliomyelitis, typhoid fever, malaria, and some forms of pneumonia has not reduced the need for doctors in the United States. People who would have died in infancy, childhood, or as young adults now survive to develop diseases of older ages such as ulcers, cancer, heart disease, and cerebral strokes, and other medical problems of old age. That sometime in the future man will be able to get along without doctors is an idea that will not come true for a long time, if ever.

Medical science can, however, aim toward the ideal of keeping individuals reasonably free from the need for medical care from early childhood to old age. Could we significantly reduce the number of sick people by advising potential parents whether or not they should have children? Not yet. Medical scientists do not know enough about human genetics to predict the genetic health of children with accuracy in more than a small percentage of cases. Only rarely can they say to a couple, "If you have a child, it is certain to have a serious disease." Neither can they say to any couple, "If you have a child, it is certain to be free from a hereditary disease." If the odds are fifty-fifty or one in four or one in eight of having a child with a genetic disease, the couple may decide against taking the risk. Most of us have relatives with diseases having a genetic basis, and perhaps all of us carry recessive genes that would cause disease if our child inherited the same defective gene from the other parent. And yet, most matings produce healthy children.

The long and short of it is that genetic counseling may be very important for some individual couples, but it is not likely to make any noticeable difference in the pool of undesirable genes in our national population or in the amount of disease for a number of years. The general reason is that most genetic defects are recessive; it is not possible to identify more than a few carriers. The use of genetic counseling will become more important when it becomes possible to detect undesirable genes in each individual prior to mating. Already this can sometimes be done by biochemical tests or by microscopic examination of the chromosomes.

It is now possible to insert a hypodermic needle into the

uterus of a pregnant woman and to draw off some of the amniotic fluid that surrounds the embryo. This procedure is called *amniocentesis*. Chemical tests of this fluid or microscopic examination of cells that are in the fluid—they may be grown in tissue culture for a time before study—will show whether the embryo bears certain genetic defects. If a serious disease is present, the embryo may be aborted. These procedures are almost completely safe. Later pregnancies in the same woman may result in healthy children. When methods already known are perfected, it will be possible to detect about 100 different inherited diseases before the embryo develops into a baby. But, as I have said before, most such diseases are rare.

There is another way in which genetic counseling benefits couples who mate. It may relieve needless worry about the risk of having defective children. For example, a healthy brother of a hemophiliac (a bleeder) may fear that his children will inherit the disease, but they cannot inherit a gene for hemophilia from a man who does not have the disease. Hemophilia is a sex-linked disease. Sex-linked heredity is any characteristic which occurs only in males or only in females. Roughly 10 percent of all diseases caused by a single defective gene are sex-linked. Hemophilia is not passed from father to son, nor does a healthy male carry the gene. It may be transmitted from an affected male to his daughters, who in turn may pass the defective gene to either daughters or sons. In order for a female to have the disease, she must inherit the gene from each parent. Males always develop the disease when they inherit the gene. Healthy male relatives of hemophiliacs frequently worry about transmitting the disease to their children, but a genetic counselor would relieve their fears.

About seventy sex-linked defects have been identified. Only a few of them are caused by dominant genes. Vitamin D-resistant rickets is an example. Some kinds of anemia are also sex-linked, as are some types of deafness, red-green color blindness, and a form of muscular dystrophy. In all sex-linked inheritance, both dominant and recessive, there is the absence of father-to-son transmission. This is because the X chromosome of the male is passed to each daughter of an affected father but never to a son.

POSITIVE EUGENICS

There is a way of reducing the number of inherited diseases which is more rapid than ordinary mating guided by genetic counseling. It is called *positive eugenics* and involves the use of artificial insemination. A man produces billions of sperm cells in his lifetime, several times the number of people on earth. Each ejaculation of semen contains millions of sperm cells. It requires only one to fertilize an egg cell and to produce a child. Semen may be collected from a healthy man and injected into the vagina of a woman at the time of ovulation, and she can become pregnant. Enough semen to contain many thousands of sperm cells is used in order to increase the chances that one will reach the egg cell. Artificial insemination is sometimes done when a husband and wife want children but the husband is sterile or it is known that he carries defective genes. The procedure should be done by a properly trained physician who carefully studies the health and family history of each sperm donor.

It has been proposed that artificial insemination be widely used to reduce the pool of undesirable genes in our national population. This might involve creating sperm banks where the sperm of carefully selected donors would be kept until withdrawn for insemination. Many people find the idea distasteful because they idealize marriage, parental pride, and love. To some, especially the young, such ideas may be old-fashioned. An increasing number of marriages do not last. Many parents fail to give time and love to their children. It is predicted that family life will disappear and that, because of the rising independence of women, they will copulate for pleasure and will welcome the opportunity to have children fathered by biologically superior sperm donors of their choosing. To the argument that positive eugenics by artificial insemination lowers man to the level of animals, it can be said that both man and lower animals mate almost randomly and with little regard for biological fitness. Only when man guides the mating of animals is the breed rapidly improved. Should not man try to do as well or better for his own species?

It has also been proposed that methods be developed for collecting and banking egg cells from women. (A sperm or an egg bank would keep them protected and nourished at low temperatures.) An egg cell might then be fertilized by a sperm cell outside the body, allowed to grow a little while, and then be implanted into the uterus of a foster mother. Human egg cells have been collected, fertilized, and allowed to grow for a number of days outside the body. Maybe it will become possible to keep the embryo growing in an artificial womb so that it develops into a baby. Then women could be free from the sometimes unwanted responsibility of pregnancy. If this proposal shocks you, don't worry about it. Medical science is nowhere near the perfection of an artificial womb. The processes of the natural growth of an embryo are almost unbelievably complex, and a great deal goes on that is not understood at all. Still, it may sometime be possible to fertilize a human egg cell outside the body and then implant it in a uterus where these complex processes of nature will grow it into a baby.

What do physicians trained in genetics think of the plan to force an extensive program of positive eugenics as a way of reducing the incidence of inherited diseases? Aside from moral issues and matters of taste, they are afraid that there would be harmful outcomes. At least a few genes that are harmful in some respects are claimed to be beneficial in others. Carriers of the recessive gene for sickle-cell anemia tend to be resistant to malaria. The selective breeding of animals for special traits has sometimes led to bad results. Horses and dogs bred for speed are likely to be nervous and not of much use for anything but racing. Some highly selected strains of rats are very susceptible to infections. Dogs bred for a number of physical and behavioral traits have some diseases and faults not found as frequently in mongrels.

Most individuals within all races of man are remarkably adaptable to changes in environment and to the kinds of learning required. The selective breeding of domestic animals into pure strains has been done for fixity of behaviors. It does not seem desirable to reduce useful differences and adaptability among human beings. These are some of the reasons why physicians trained in genetics say that there is risk of causing more harm than good by fooling around with the genes of man. Although it seems desirable to reduce the biological causes of diseases and of incompetence very few medical scientists want to force an extensive program of artificial insemination on the people of any group.

On the other hand, there seems to be little risk in the

voluntary practice of artificial insemination when it is requested by a wife and husband. This practice already exists and could be increased according to gains in knowledge and attitudes towards parenthood. It does not involve a risk of breeding desirable traits out of a population. The voluntary practice of artificial insemination is very different from the proposal to build a super race by forcing a population to practice positive eugenics.

A few medical scientists say that there is no need to reduce the pool of defective genes in the whole population because it is going to be possible to cure all the inherited diseases. Maybe so, but I am sure that is not going to be soon. At present no inherited disease can be completely cured in all the patients that have it. We sometimes hear or read that insulin cures all diabetics, but this is not true. Insulin does not cure; it controls the symptoms and the metabolic disorders of the disease. Most diabetic patients do not like to follow a strict diet or to take insulin. Some of them live happily and well for a normal span of life. Others, for unknown reasons, develop serious complications. It seems probable that it will always be better to prevent a disease than to try to cure it or control it after it has developed.

Some biologists and physicians predict that within five or ten years it will become possible to repair defective genes or to replace them with normal genes. It has become possible to make some bacterial genes and to transfer small blocks of genes from one bacterium to another. It is predicted that this can be done with human genes, but it will be a very difficult process. Even if it becomes possible to repair and replace individual genes, it is unlikely that diseases caused by several defective genes (polygenic diseases) could be corrected by such methods. I do not say that these predictions will never come true, but I will wager odds that it will require longer than the five to ten years that are sometimes predicted. Should these procedures become possible, it will be necessary to test them carefully over long periods of time to learn of any bad results.

All cells of the body contain the same set of genes that are found in the beginning fertilized egg cell. They are suppressed in ordinary cells so that they are not working to grow a new individual. But in some lower organisms —frogs, salamanders, and fruit flies—it has become possible to replace the nucleus of a fertilized egg with the nucleus of an ordinary cell and have the egg grow into an organism. In the experiment on frogs, the nucleus of the fertilized egg is replaced with the nucleus of a blood cell from another frog. The egg cell grows into a frog which is genetically identical with the frog from which the blood cell was taken. This process is called *cloning*.

It may become possible to clone human beings. According to the predictions of some people who think boldly about the future, it will become possible to take cells from the body of a man and grow an exact copy of him, dozens or hundreds of times. It might become possible to take cells from the body of a child killed in an accident—some cells live for hours after the heart stops beating—culture them and grow an exact genetic copy of the dead child. Or a woman might obtain a few cells from her favorite movie star and have a copy of him grown in her body. There are all sorts of wild possibilities. But it is also possible that cloning will not work in humans. Higher organisms are more likely to reject substances or tissues from another person. It has not yet been shown that genes from ordinary human cells will "turn on" when placed in a fertilized egg. Even if the embryo should grow, it might become defective. If cloning works in man, it offers a possible way to reduce genetic defects: just clone from people of proven health and competence. There are arguments that cloning should not be tried in man, and I shall review them in a chapter on the ethics of selective population control.

I believe that we should encourage and support the training of doctors to do genetic counseling; we should also support research to improve the detection of carriers of defective genes and to judge the risk of disease for each couple proposing to have children. We should encourage newspapers, magazines, radio, and television to tell about the possible benefits of genetic counseling. It could grow into an important field of preventive medicine.

An increased number of people could live a normal life span and have fewer diseases if everyone carefully applied all that is now known about preventing diseases. If people did not smoke or use addictive drugs, if they used only moderate amounts of alcohol, if clean air and water and good sanitation were available to all, if people ate only needed amounts of good foods, and if they exercised properly, human bodies would last longer. But our imperfections extend to behavior as well, and many of us are like the poetess who wrote

> My candle burns at both ends;
> It will not last the night;
> But, ah, my foes, and, oh, my friends—
> It gives a lovely light!
> *Edna St. Vincent Millay**

* From COLLECTED POEMS, Harper & Row. Copyright 1922, 1950 by Edna St. Vincent Millay. By permission of Norma Millay Ellis.

IV

Intelligence

General intelligence is the ability to learn ideas and to do abstract reasoning. It is made up of a number of more specific abilities. People differ greatly in intelligence, ranging from idiocy to genius. Heredity is of great importance in determining the level of intelligence that each individual is able to develop out of environmental experiences.

An idiot cannot learn to speak, read, count, or care for himself. He can sometimes be toilet trained and learn to respond to simple commands but that is about all. Severe retardates are unable to progress in regular schools and may be placed in special schools for training or just custodial care. They can learn to speak and do simple things but are unable to earn a living. Each needs a guardian. Children who are moderately retarded may progress a little way in school but not out of the grades unless their teachers promote them without significant achievement. Advancement in school does not prove that a child is normal in ability to learn, and failure to advance in school does not prove that a child is stupid.

Most children are about average in intelligence; they are capable of advancing into high school and many of them complete high school. An increasing number attend college, and about 50 percent of those who enter graduate from college. A smaller number are very bright and learn easily. Very few belong to the genius class. A genius may find school work easy, but an occasional one does poorly because he finds it dull and boring.

The Testing of Intelligence

Intelligence tests consist of different kinds of short tasks, commonly done with paper and pencil, that require reasoning. They are not the same as tests of information, although some kinds of basic information are needed for reasoning. Intelligence tests were developed by trying out thousands and thousands of short tests and selecting those that discriminated best between dull and bright students and between those judged to be mentally retarded and those judged to be normal or brighter than average.

There are other means of selecting items for the tests. Most of these involve statistical analyses and are rather complicated. After spending the first twenty years developing, improving, and checking these tests, many psychologists became very proud of them and began to claim and that they measured inherited intelligence very accurately. During the past 40 years this conclusion has been questioned over and over. The tests have never been perfect, but in my opinion they are very useful. A number of people, some psychologists among them, now claim that intelligence tests are worthless and should not be used. It is my impression that the people who say this do not know very much about the development and validation of these tests and reject them because they do not want to accept conclusions based on data from intelligence tests. For example, critics say that intelligence tests were standardized on native-born, middle-class schoolchildren and are not fair to children of other backgrounds and cultures. It is true that most of the testing was done on normal students in good schools, but during the development of the tests they were also used on large numbers of retarded and underprivileged children.

Psychologists have developed an expression of intelligence called the Intelligence Quotient, or IQ for short. It is not measured directly by tests but is calculated by dividing the actual age of the child into its mental age and then multiplying by 100. (In recent years psychologists have stopped doing these calculations and take IQ values from standardized tables. My discussion here illustrates the meaning of IQ and how it was calculated up to about 1960.) Remember that the word "quotient" comes from arithmetic and is a value obtained by dividing one number into another. Psychologists first tested children of all ages on intelligence tests. They picked the average test score at each age to represent the normal, or norm, for that age. Suppose that the test score of a child is at the norm for 12-year-olds. We say that the child has a mental age of 12 years. The actual age of the child is 10; he has done better than the average child of his age. We divide the mental age 12 by the actual age 10 and multiply by 100: $\frac{12}{10} \times 100 = 120$. We then say that the child has an Intelligence Quotient, or IQ, of 120. He is brighter than average; the average IQ is 100. Actually, I should have said that according to the test, he is brighter than average.

As a second example suppose that a child of 14 years has a mental age of 7—his score is at the average level for

7-year-olds. We calculate his IQ by: $\frac{7}{14} \times 100 = 50$. It is below average; according to the test the child is mentally retarded—quite severely so.

If the child is average in intelligence-test performance, the IQ is about 100; if the child is above average, the IQ is higher than 100; and if the child is below average, the IQ is lower than 100. However, the development of ability to perform on intelligence tests levels off at about age 16. So psychologists do not use ages higher than 16 in calculating IQ. If a man having an actual age of 60 has a tested mental age of 15, the calculation $\frac{15}{60} \times 100 = 25$ would make the man seem to be an idiot. Recalculate it using the figure 16 as the highest testable mental age—$\frac{15}{16} \times 100 = 94$—and the answer falls within the normal range.

When psychologists study the distribution of IQs for the whole population, they find that most of them cluster around 100 and the number falls off as you move either above or below the average. There are very few people with an IQ near zero, and there are very few as high as 200.

There are many different forms of intelligence tests. An IQ calculated from the results of one test generally agrees closely with the IQ calculated for the same person from the results of a different test. There is a good reason for this. Each psychologist who constructs a new test is likely to check it against some highly respected test such as the Stanford-Binet. If the results do not agree closely, he is likely to modify his test until they do. Only rarely does anyone try to develop a new test of intelligence from scratch, using new ideas and methods. Some scientists have tried to find a direct way of estimating intelligence as by measuring reaction time, brain waves, speed of nerve conduction, and the like, but all have been unsuccessful thus far.

Intelligence tests seem to work pretty well. When the same individual is retested, the IQ is reasonably constant. This is not true of the very young child, for his brain has not yet matured. But by the time a child reaches school, his IQ begins to stabilize. The IQ is useful in predicting school and job success. When the IQ is low, it is almost certain that the child will not progress very far in school. When the IQ is high, the child is much more likely to do well in school but does not always do so. A common reason is that he or she dislikes school. The IQ falls when severe brain injuries occur or when large amounts of certain parts of the brain are removed by surgery or are destroyed by disease. The IQ also falls when an aging person develops senility, for many cells of the brain then become diseased or are destroyed.

Intelligence tests are not good measures of the creativity and originality of the child. A child with a low IQ is almost never creative, but neither are most children with high IQs, although almost all creative individuals do have a higher-than-average IQ. There are other important abilities that intelligence tests do not measure well. The IQ is not a good measure of artistic or musical ability, clerical or mechanical aptitude. There are other tests of these special abilities, and some of them work very well. To have a high IQ does not mean that the person is good at writing stories, poetry, or plays, designing clothes, buildings, or machines; the IQ is not a measure of these special abilities. It is intended to be a general measure of ability to learn abstract ideas and to reason with them.

Some professors and social and political leaders do not wish to accept the idea that individuals differ in the genetic bases of intelligence. Our Constitution states that all men are created equal. This is a very appealing and popular idea. It is useful to politicians and social reformers who are trying to attract followers. If all men are equal at birth in respect to the genes they inherit, it then follows that all differences in achievement in later life represent social injustices. It is probable that our Founding Fathers referred to equality at birth as meaning equal rights as citizens. Most of us accept the principle of equal rights and freedoms for all men. But the idea that individuals are all biologically equal at birth is obviously not true.

Although intelligence is just one of several important traits of personality, it is basic to school and job success and advancement. For this reason I emphasize the importance of intelligence in this book.

THE ROLE OF ENVIRONMENT

Biological factors in the environment affect the individual from the time the egg is fertilized and begins to divide and grow. Even when the fertilized egg splits into two and develops identical twins—they are identical only in respect to the genes they carry—one twin gains an advantage over the other in respect to position in the uterus; at birth one twin is usually a little heavier than the other. Also, the nutrients and hormones that mothers supply to embryos are not identical. If a mother uses addictive drugs, her baby may be born an addict. Sometimes a substance carried through the blood of the mother causes a birth defect in the child; when the brain is involved, the child may be mentally retarded. Not all causes of birth defects are known. As noted earlier, some are caused by defective genes.

Many fertilized egg cells fail to develop into babies. The fertilized egg may never get attached to the wall of the uterus, or it may become attached and then something goes wrong and it is destroyed. This is Nature's way of taking care of many of the problems that develop in the uterus, and we should not regret the end of a pregnancy that might have produced a defective baby. There is no more need to sorrow over the loss of these beginning lives than over the billions of living sperm from each man and the few hundred living ova from each woman that perish rather than develop into people. Aborted embryos cease to exist before they become conscious of self and develop a will to live.

There are disorders of pregnancy that cause a baby to be delivered prematurely. It is sometimes possible to prevent a miscarriage, or if a premature birth occurs after seven months of pregnancy have passed, it is commonly possible to save the baby so that it grows into a healthy child.

The nutrition of a mother can affect an embryo, but not to the extent that some people imagine. First, when undernutrition is extreme the woman does not ovulate and therefore cannot become pregnant. And second, if an undernourished woman becomes pregnant, her body will mobilize its own proteins to nourish the embryo. Following birth her body will still do its best to supply proteins for milk. But there are levels of starvation that permit pregnancy, starve the baby before birth, and supply too little milk for it after birth. When there is too little protein in early life, the brain does not develop normally, it may be permanently damaged, and the child becomes mentally retarded. Most of us saw television and newspaper pictures of the horrible cases of starving mothers, babies, and children in Biafra and in East Pakistan during the recent wars. These were examples of protein-deficiency disease.

Does such severe starvation occur in America? It does in some individuals although it has not been proven to occur frequently, even in slums. But there are many poor people who are undernourished or who do not eat a well-balanced diet. Some eat harmful substances such as lead paint. Many others who can afford a well-balanced diet do not eat one or eat too much. Do these milder states of undernutrition and malnutrition affect the development of the brain and hence of intelligence of a child? It has been claimed that this is true, but it has not been proven, for the evidence is indirect. The average intelligence of slum populations is lower than the national average, and some of those living in slums eat a substandard diet. But the association of two factors does not prove a cause-and-effect-relationship. It may be that lower-than-average intelligence leads to poverty and hence to poor nutrition. This is the sort of question that can be settled only by further research.

There have been many studies of acute starvation in adults. For religious reasons, or by being a faddist, a political protester, or a scientist studying the effects of starvation, many individuals have starved themselves to the point of death. A few have done this over and over. Fasting has not been shown to permanently harm the brain or to lower the intelligence of adults. During starvation the brain is the last tissue of the body to give up its protein. But in early life, when the brain is growing rapidly it must have adequate amounts of protein.

The brains of some children are injured at birth. In the past some doctors were too rough when they aided the delivery of a baby by holding it around the head with forceps. Some brain-damaged children are mentally retarded; others are handicapped in controlling their muscles but are of normal intelligence. The effects of birth injury depend on the parts of the brain that are damaged. Babies are sometimes deprived of oxygen during birth or later in life, as when they narrowly escape drowning. Brain cells are damaged quickly by lack of oxygen. There are diseases that cause brain damage; they, too, are among the biological factors in the environment that can lower intelligence.

It is claimed that a number of social factors have permanent effects on intelligence. Some studies on laboratory animals, such as rats and mice, show that when young are raised in an environment that provides a lot of stimulation—a so-called "enriched" environment—the brains grow larger than in similar animals kept in isolation. Other studies show that having the young animal do a lot of learning also causes the brain to grow larger. These claims are very interesting and may be correct, but some critics say that the studies have not been well controlled and that it has not been proven that animals raised in an enriched environment are permanently improved in ability to learn.

Does enrichment of a child's environment cause an increase in his IQ? Yes; in the average child, there is at least a temporary increase. But it has not been shown that there is any lasting effect on his IQ or on school performance. In the very young child the brain has not matured, it learns relatively few abstract ideas, and it does relatively little abstract reasoning. Because measures of intelligence at an early age are not very reliable or stable, the results of enrichment at an early age are equally questionable. (I shall say more about efforts to raise IQ in later sections of this chapter.)

When a child is not given the tools of reasoning, such as language, numbers, and pictures, he or she cannot do well on tests that require their use. Children who have been raised in the almost complete absence of social experiences perform very poorly on intelligence tests. But those who have normal brains show dramatic increases in IQ when placed in a good environment at a later time.

It is frequently claimed that intelligence tests were designed and standardized on middle-class children and that children raised in slum cultures use different words and have different meanings for common words. Therefore, the tests do not accurately measure the intelligence of slum children. There is truth in this criticism, but children from other countries quickly learn our language and do well on intelligence tests. It seems likely that many children of the slums—not all—were born to parents whose capacity to learn was low and who were thus unable to get good jobs that would permit them to live outside the slum. Therefore, it would be the level of inherited intelligence rather than the anomalies of slum culture that cause slum children to do badly on intelligence tests.

There is also a theory that just being poor is destructive to intelligence, spirit, and ambition, and that the brain itself can be harmed by it. There is no hard evidence to support this theory. There is, however, a partial test of the theory when slum families are broken up and brothers and sisters are raised apart, some in an enriched environment and some in a deprived environment. Adopted children continue to resemble their true parents much more than they resemble their foster parents. I shall say more of such studies.

THE ROLE OF HEREDITY

Animals have been bred selectively for intelligent behavior. Some breeds of dogs, for example, are good at different kinds of hunting. The behavior of deer- and wolfhounds is very different from that of setters, pointers, and retrievers, who aid their masters in hunting birds. That rat terrier is no good at trailing large game but excels at locating and digging for little animals that live in holes. None of these hunting dogs is useful for herding sheep and cattle, but the collie and several breeds of shepherd dogs may be trained to remarkable skills in managing flocks. The Pekingese and several lap dogs have no aptitude for any of these activities, although they can learn some tricks and can learn to obey a number of commands.

Rats have been bred selectively for ability to learn a maze. After a few generations they become separated into "bright" and "dull" strains, and it may be shown by crossbreeding that the trait is inherited and seems to involve several genes. It is misleading to generalize about these animals as being "bright" and "dull," for the ability to learn a maze is highly specific. When the two strains are tested for other types of learning, they do not differ very much. Learning to run a maze is not a measure of ability to learn abstract ideas and to do abstract reasoning. Human beings are not much better than rats at learning a maze.

Finally there are scientists who argue that the inheritance of physical traits in animals and in man and the inheritance of abilities in animals do not mean a thing when we consider the heritability of human intelligence. They suppose that the human brain, the most advanced product of human evolution, is not subject to the laws of heredity. They claim that all healthy children are born with the same genetic potential for the development of intelligence.

It is difficult to prove just how much heredity and environment each contribute to human intelligence. The contributions may differ greatly among individuals. When a child inherits a tiny or malformed brain, no amount of training or enrichment of the environment will overcome this genetic handicap. At the other extreme, suppose that a baby from bright parents almost drowns in the bathtub and his brain is badly damaged from being without oxygen for a few minutes. This biological cause of mental retardation is environmental. Either environmental or genetic factors may cause idiocy, and no genetic or environmental way is known to make a dull or average child into a genius.

What about the importance of heredity in determining the intelligence of people who appear to be physically normal? It has been observed for a long time that intelligence tends to run in families. This does not prove, however, that biological heredity is responsible, for intelligent parents are likely to live in a good environment. The environmentalists claim that children of bright parents become bright because of good home culture, good nutrition, good schools, and pressure from the parents to succeed.

Studies have been done on adopted children raised in advantaged homes. It was found that a well-educated couple is likely to adopt a child only when it is known that the true parents are intelligent and of good health. The illegitimate baby of healthy university students is likely to be in great demand for adoption. Adoption agencies try to place bright, healthy babies in the best homes, and they try to place them according to race, nationality, religion, and physical characteristics. A blond baby is likely to be placed with blond parents. With this much selection, it is not surprising that good foster parents tend to have bright, healthy foster children.

Researchers aware of selective adoption have attempted to study adoptions where the IQ of the true parents, the child, its brothers and sisters, and that of the foster parents could be determined. They have done follow-up studies on brothers and sisters who were adopted into different homes, some into an enriched environment and some into a deprived environment. The general outcome of these studies was that adopted children were found to be much more like their true parents than like their foster parents in respect to intelligence. Such studies are not the best possible. Brothers and sisters are not identical in respect to the genes they inherit. They may even inherit traits from grandparents that do not appear in their parents.

A number of scientists interested in the inheritance of human intelligence and personality have studied identical and ordinary twins reared together and reared apart in different kinds of environments. Ordinary twins—they come from two separate egg cells that just happened to get fertilized at the same time—are no more alike than ordinary brothers and sisters. Identical twins arose from one fertilized egg that splits into two individuals so that each twin gets identical genes. It is commonly supposed that identical twins are biologically identical after they develop into babies, but this is not so; Nature makes no two living things exactly alike. They are similar but not identical. Cars are never alike even when built from the same blueprint. Nature, like the machinist, tolerates small differences in the building process so that the final products are never exactly identical. I emphasize this point because environmentalists are likely to attribute all differences between identical twins to differences in the social environment. Physical and biological differences in the environment are important, too, although we do not know how much they affect intelligence and personality. It is not accurate to speak of "identical" twins; we should follow the recommendation of Professor Roger J. Williams and use the expression "one-egg" twins. Studies of one-egg twins show that there is generally not much change in intelligence when they are reared apart in different environments. The environmental effect on IQ is striking in a few individuals, but the average change is small.

Intelligence tests are indirect measures of intelligence. It should not be assumed that a change in IQ or a difference in IQ is always a true measure of the ability of the brain to do abstract reasoning. An apparent environmental effect on IQ may sometimes be more of a mistake or an error of measurement than a true change in intelligence. Environment sometimes gets undeserved credit for apparent changes in intelligence.

On the basis of the evidence, it has been estimated that genetic factors account for at least twice as much of the variation in IQ as do environmental factors. It is not possible to be exact in judging the importance of these factors. One problem is that there are not as many twin studies as would be desirable. Maybe heredity is more important than this estimate indicates, and maybe its relative importance is less.

The environmentalists are not convinced that heredity is important. On one hand, they claim that intelligence tests are worthless. On the other, they emphasize the occasional large difference in the IQs of one-egg twins reared apart and ignore the fact that the average difference is small—only a little larger than the average difference in IQs of one-egg twins raised together. In my opinion many of those who claim that environment is all-important are poorly trained in the methods of science, for they exhibit many logical and statistical fallacies in their reasoning and their research studies are usually poorly designed and controlled.

It has been claimed over and over that special training of mentally retarded children can raise their IQs to near normal or to normal. It is true that the average IQ of retarded children can be increased by special training. I emphasize "average" for in some individual cases the IQ falls a bit despite training. Moreover, in most instances an improvement does not last when special training is stopped. Sometimes the special training is little more than coaching the child how to perform well on intelligence tests. It just is not possible—not yet, anyway—to turn mentally retarded children into average or bright children by either enrichment of the environment or by special training. If environment is of major importance in determining the level of intelligence, it should be possible to permanently raise an IQ over quite a range by improving the environment. But that does not happen. This is one sort of evidence that heredity is more important than environment in determining the level of intelligence.

There is another kind of evidence for the importance of heredity. In a study of more than 80,000 individuals having IQs lower than 69, it was found that their families had a high incidence of mental retardation. Almost 50 percent of the retardates had either one or both parents retarded. A larger number had close relatives who were retarded. About 10 percent of the retardates had been brain-damaged by such diseases as meningitis, encephalitis, poliomyelitis, congenital syphilis, birth injuries, and accidental injuries to the brain. There remains, however, a large group of retardates who have neither a family history of retardation nor any obvious environmental cause. The cause of such mental retardation remains a medical mystery.

Although some social scientists claim that mental retardation is caused by a poor social environment, this is not accepted by all medical scientists who work with retarded children. There are a number of children who have been kept isolated in locked rooms or closets and are sometimes chained or tied for long periods of time. Such children are likely to perform poorly on intelligence tests when first removed from their cruel environment for they lack experience with language, numbers, and pictures and so lack practice in reasoning with them. Some of these children are true retardates, others are mentally ill without true retardation, and others are unmanageable autistic children. Sometimes stories are published about wild children who have raised with animals—"wolf-children." Such stories are not true; they get started because of the animal-like behavior of autistic children. Unless an isolated child is a true retardate, however, he is likely to perform better on intelligence tests after being placed in a normal environment. This is one sort of evidence that social isolation does not doom a child to have a low IQ for the rest of his life.

I shall now describe two of several genetic diseases that cause mental retardation. The first is Down's syndrome, named for the physician who first described it. The word "syndrome" means the set symptoms of a disease that are commonly found together. The disease is also called Mongoloid idiocy, only because the eyes of patients bear a little resemblance to the eyes of Mongolian people. Not all of these patients are severely retarded; a few are only moderately so. It is now known that the genetic basis of this disease involves the chromosomes rather than a single gene within a chromosome. Chromosomes are normally grouped in pairs that are referred to by number. In most cases of Down's syndrome, there are three chromosomes instead of two at position twenty-one. In some other patients, the mixing up of chromosomes is a little more complicated. Human geneticists are also beginning to understand why women who become pregnant at an older age—such as past forty—are more likely than young women to have children with Down's syndrome. This disease occurs about once in every 500 births (some estimates are once in every 600 or 700 births). Since most of these patients do not live very long or are sometimes sterile, they seldom have children. But some do reproduce and pass on this chromosomal defect.

The second disease is a simple recessive genetic defect called phenylketonuria (PKU for short), which is estimated to occur about once in every 8000 births. When a word ends in "-uria," it usually refers to urine. This disease gets its name because of the large amount of phenylpyruvic acid in the urine. It is easy to test for this condition at the time a child is born, and some states require that this be done. The defective gene causes the absence of an enzyme that helps the body use an amino acid called phenylalanine (amino acids are joined together to make proteins). When the body cannot use phenylalanine in a normal way, some abnormal substances are formed that damage the brain. One of these abnormal compounds is phenylpyruvic acid. PKU is treated by feeding the patient foods that have little phenylalanine. This avoids brain damage in some children but is not a fully effective treatment in all of them.

When mentally retarded individuals reproduce, they may have mentally retarded children. They do not always, even when they carry genes for retardation. Most defective genes are recessive, and for a child to develop the disorder, it is necessary to inherit the same recessive gene from each parent. Some forms of mental retardation are probably caused by more than one defective gene working together, and this complicates the tracing of mental retardation in families. Parents of average or above-average intelligence might have a retarded child because it has inherited the same recessive gene or genes from each parent. Many cases of mental retardation are not known to be hereditary; the causes of some cases of retardation are unknown.

When mentally retarded individuals reproduce, they tend to have larger than average families. Some people are gravely concerned about the possibility that retardates are outbreeding people of average and above-average intelligence. The fact is, however, that many retardates remain childless. Idiots and severe retardates almost never mate; even some of the moderately retarded remain childless. But when they do copulate, they are not likely to practice birth control, so they tend to have large families. They commonly lack an understanding of reproduction and methods of birth control, and there has been little effort to bring the needed information and services to them. It does not seem to be true that retardates are outbreeding normal people.

The Future

It has been estimated that if all retardates remained childless, it would be possible to reduce the number of retarded children in this country to half in one generation. The basis for this estimate is that about half the retardates in the United States have at least one retarded parent. This estimate is disputed, but it may be close to being right. There are approximately four million (*2* percent of the population) people in our country with an IQ under 70. Some estimates place the figure as high as six million (3 percent of the population). It is estimated that another fourteen million have an IQ between 70 and 80.

Most retardates are unable to provide a good home for children and to give them adequate care. Some of our states have laws against the marriage of the mentally retarded, but these laws have not been enforced. What about people who are borderline between retardates and those of average intelligence? I refer to a range of 70 to 85 in IQ, the so-called "dull normals." Individuals in this range are more likely than normals to be jobless, to get into trouble with the law, to be school failures, and to be poor parents. It does seem to me that many of them should be encouraged to remain childless but not merely on the basis of an IQ test.

Should society encourage the breeding of genius? In the future, it will be possible to have sperm banks and perhaps egg-cell banks to preserve the genes of our most brilliant men and women. There is the risk, however, that a population selected for high intelligence might have an increased number of defects. I know no one trained in medical genetics who wants to take the risk involved in trying to breed a race that is superior in one trait. It seems to many of us that most average people are competent in jobs, parenthood, health, and citizenship and that the common sense of many is needed together with the genius of the few.

But mental retardation is a major cause of human misery and of social problems. Should not all retardates be encouraged to remain childless?

V

Education

One of the ideals that guides our present national, state, and local planning for education is that every child should have good schooling. For a long time this country did not invest much money and effort toward achieving that ideal. There were poor public schools in city slums, isolated rural areas, and especially in neighborhoods made up of minority groups. Most good schools were in middle- and upper-class neighborhoods. In general the quality of a school was determined by what the residents of a neighborhood were willing and able to pay for it.

Between the years 1953 and 1969 our expenditures for public schools and colleges increased from about 8.5 billion dollars per year to more than 49 billion dollars per year. Many new schools were built in disadvantaged areas with state and federal funds. It was expected that improved education would be the answer to poverty. For some disadvantaged children this was true. They were able to do well in school and escape a deprived environment. But there was surprise and dismay when it was found that most disadvantaged children continued to lag behind national norms in school achievement. Some parents blamed the teachers and school administrators and asked for local control of the schools, but most of these parents, especially in slums, fail to act wisely when they gain control of a school. There have been many attempts to shift the blame for the continued educational lag from one group to another. But only a few educators have dared to more than whisper that many children do poorly in school because they are of low intelligence, although it is acknowledged that children may lack motivation to study because of the negative attitudes they learn within their family and neighborhood.

By 1965, costly programs of compensatory education were begun and more than a billion dollars per year has been spent on Headstart and similar programs. These attempts to improve the school performance of disadvantaged children have failed in most instances.

It was also found that there is little, if any, relationship between the amount of money spent per pupil and his or her school achievement. This was the conclusion reached as the result of extensive studies of cost-quality in American public schools. It was published in the Coleman report (J. S. Coleman, et al. *Equality of Educational Opportunity*. U.S. Department of Health, Education, and Welfare. Office of Education, Washington, D.C., 1966). This too brought cries of dismay and frantic attempts to place the blame. I am reminded of the old rhyme:

> When in error, when in doubt,
> Run in circles, yell and shout.

But it is not funny.

THE ROLE OF ENVIRONMENT

Jewish children in the United States have an average IQ about eight points above the national average. They generally do well in school and in jobs. Jews have contributed a great deal to discovery and creativity. And yet in the recent past many of them were subjected to cruel discrimination and were forced to live in slums. Many of them attended poorly equipped and staffed schools. Is there something in the culture of the Jews that encourages them to work hard to overcome environmental handicaps? Indeed there is! When I was talking with a Jewish friend about this, he said, "Don't you know that Jewish mothers put honey on books?" Most Jewish children are encouraged by their families to read, get a good education, and to work hard. Asians—also subjected to discrimination in America—also have a culture that encourages the child to learn.

The cultural environment is very different in Appalachia, where there is little encouragement to learn more than to read, write, and do simple arithmetic. There, many individuals, perhaps most of them, are without hope that they can do better. When these families move to cities, they can afford nothing better than slum housing. The culture of the alley is no better than that of the hills. It is that of school indifference, delinquency, crime, alcohol, and drugs.

Some of the Communist countries have taken sweeping measures to improve the cultural environment of the child. In most families both parents are employed. Soon after weaning a child, the mother returns to her job and the infant spends his or her days in a nursery. He or she progresses into child and youth programs that take

up most of the waking hours with useful activities. There
are extensive sports programs. The children are with
their parents during evening hours and on weekends.
Well-trained professionals run these programs. The children are kept away from opportunities to learn delinquency, and every effort is made to motivate them to
progress as far as they are able in schools. They are
placed in schools according to drives and abilities. Of
course one of the primary objectives of a Communist
government is to train the children to be good passive
communists. They are not encouraged or even permitted
to speak for themselves on political matters.

In Israel, the kibbutzim offer another form of child
rearing that motivates the young to do their best and
to become good citizens. These are collective-farm set-
tlements in which children are raised in communes. If
you are interested in the ways that they function and
the results of this general method of child rearing, I
recommend that you read *The Children of the Dream*
by Bruno Bettelheim (see Suggested Readings, page
140).

If we in the United States took such measures to give
all children a good cultural environment and to motivate
them to study, there is risk that our bureaucrats would
aim for thought control as well. Many think that our
political leaders and bureaucrats already have too much
power over our individual lives. Although I like the idea
of programs providing useful, healthful activities for
children all day long, I do not know how we can achieve
such a socialistic program without giving up some of
our cherished freedoms.

The Headstart programs are a move toward improving the cultural environment of the very young child.
Some of the groups that have studied the results of these

programs claim that they have failed completely. There is a temporary improvement in the test performance and school achievement of the average child, but when these children are placed in regular schools with children who have not been in Headstart, they soon lose their advantage. Critics say that the Headstart programs were got together in haste with too little experience, too little planning, and with too few competent teachers to run them. In many instances the children spend their time at simple activities which have little to do with learning. Some psychologists say that the cultural environment of the disadvantaged child must be changed in infancy and that the first few years are vital in determining how well a child will do in school. It may be that if Headstart programs were begun earlier and continued longer they would have a lasting benefit.

The development of these catch-up, or Headstart-like, programs should have started with research on methods and with expertly planned pilot studies. Congress and our leaders in education were pressured into trying to provide instant solutions to the problems of the disadvantaged. There was a lot of ballyhoo about the apparent early success of some programs, especially in large cities. People were merely fooled by temporary improvement. They expected it to last and began to boast. It did not last.

A number of carefully planned programs of aids to disadvantaged children have been quietly going on in the schools of education and social service in some of our universities. One such study has been conducted by Professor Fred L. Strodbeck, a sociologist at the University of Chicago. His results seem to show that it is frequently possible to benefit the disadvantaged child by special training and that the benefit sometimes lasts. But the results are not spectacular.

Many of our school systems are under attack because they have failed to abolish the achievement gap between children who come from slums and those who come from middle and upper socio-economic classes. The disadvantaged children become frustrated and sometimes turn their aggressions toward teachers, society, and even school buildings. They see no reason to have faith in education and are attracted to a culture that offers escape by alcohol, drugs, gangs, crime, and rebellion. They escape into enslavement by this sort of culture. When the young get a voice in school programs, they demand and frequently get unearned promotions, noncompetitive courses, and the dropping of grading.

Is it not probable that a major cause of the turmoil in our schools is the belief that every child is born equal in ability to learn, reason, and progress in school and that individual differences in success are caused solely by social injustices? Is it not probable that the most important cause of differences in achievement is genetic? I do not imply that genetic handicaps are the only cause of school and job failures. There are many individuals who inherit the genes for normal intelligence and drives but are handicapped by their environment. There are injustices based on the social inheritance of wealth, power, and privileges. Environmental influences are vital to success, but they must have a genetic basis on which to work.

THE ROLE OF HEREDITY

If heredity is important in determining the level of intelligence and if the level of intelligence is important in determining school success, it is reasonable to suppose that heredity is important in determining school success. Most children, not all, who fail to progress in school have low IQs. Almost all pupils who are successful in school and continue to college and professional education have higher-than-average IQs. On the other hand, not all people having a high IQ get good grades in school or go on to college. Some are not interested in school, and others have to quit school and take jobs to support a family. Some of these people become self-educated and live happy, successful lives.

Furthermore, family relationship is visible in school success. The closer the relationship of two people, the more alike they are, on the average, in school performance.

If the alternative hypothesis that environment is all-important is correct, it should be possible to permanently improve the school performance of disadvantaged children by improving the schools. After his extensive research of the problem, Professor James S. Coleman reported, "The evidence revealed that within broad geographic regions, and for each racial and ethnic group, the physical and economic resources going into a school had very little relationship to the achievements coming out of it."

A review of New York City schools showed that they have about the same enrollment as twenty-five years ago. The number of teachers has doubled, costs have increased eight times, but the pupils in these schools have slipped further and further behind national norms in school achievement. This probably reflects the movement of middle- and upper-class families to the suburbs and their replacement by disadvantaged migrant families.

It has been observed over and over that the placing of bright children into slum schools and neighborhoods does not destroy their abilities. Sometimes very intelligent young couples live in slum areas in order to have low-cost housing while going to school. Their children almost always excel in school. This sort of evidence for the importance of heredity is not convincing because the child usually lives in an enriched cultural environment within the home.

There is another factor involved, and that is drive. Drive and ambition sound like very simple functions but they are really complex. It is possible to selectively breed animals for activity drive. This is done by placing the animal in an activity wheel and recording the number of times it turns the wheel each day. Some laboratory rats just sit, eat, and sleep. Others run an average of several miles per day. Although it may seem unbelievable that the record for a rat is more than forty-five miles in a day, it does not require much energy for a rat to turn a well-balanced, oiled wheel. Strains of "active" and "inactive" rats were developed by selective breeding so that after six or seven generations all the rats in the active strain did more running than any of the rats in the inactive strain. When these animals were tested for behavior such as sex drive, hunger drive, and exploratory drive, the strain differences (activity drive) did not hold very well for other drives. There was little relationship between the strength of one drive and the strength of another drive.

There is some evidence that laziness and ambition have a genetic basis in human beings, but the question is more complicated than for lower animals. Some children who are lazy at home and in school become hard-working, successful adults. Some very bright, industrious students fizzle out as adults and stop trying to succeed. People tend to work for material rewards, but the opportunities for rewards differ according to where people are born and where they live.

THE FUTURE

What I have already said about discouraging retardates and the mentally dull from having children could be repeated here, but there is no need to elaborate on this until I begin to discuss the general problem of population control. I consider it probable that many children fail in school because they are of low intelligence and that no amount of extra effort and money is going to enable them to keep up with normal and bright children.

In the Greek story of Procrustes, the giant who seized travelers, he tied them to his bed and then trimmed off the legs of the tall or stretched the short so that all of them were made to fit the bed. If someone speaks of a Procrustean bed, he is referring to a system that forces each individual to conform to it; it is the opposite of a system that adjusts itself to suit the needs of the individual. Our educational system was once aimed to meet the widely differing needs and interests of each individual. This was an ideal that was not commonly achieved. But it was recognized that there are wide individual differences in intelligence, interests, and drives. It was known that the majority of young people were not interested in attending college but could profit from trade and vocational schools, adult education, and aids to self-education. I believe that the aim to attend to individuality was sound. Unfortunately, it was not practiced everywhere. Racial segregation was formed in the South and was encouraged in most large cities. The schools attended by minority groups were generally neglected.

Until the 1930s some Southern states did not even have high schools for Negroes.

Since the idea has become fashionable that all people are born with equal potential for developing intelligence and drives, we have moved toward trying to make all children conform to the same school system. I do not mean that everyone is being forced to take the same courses; there are still many choices of courses in high schools and colleges. However, I do agree with critics of the contemporary efforts by educators to prepare everyone for college and to encourage everyone to attend college.

In the beginning of this chapter I said that the country is spending more than 49 billion dollars per year on public schools and colleges. In fact, it is spending more. If we add the direct and indirect costs of all forms of education, including private schools and research on education, the figure exceeds 90 billion dollars per year in 1972. The United States Office of Education has estimated that in the United States there are 24 million people of eighteen years and older who cannot read, write, or count at the fifth-grade level. Most school systems are demanding more and more money to solve our crisis in education. It is estimated that children already born will double the number of students in our colleges within the next twelve years.

Isn't it time to stop wasting money on new gimmicks and new theories in education and wait until each has been carefully tested in pilot studies? What is the evidence that every man can be made a success by forcing him through college? The Scots, who are a wise, thrifty people, have a saying, "Never run after a bus, a woman, or an educational theory. There will be another along in a moment."

VI

Crime

This is going to be a short chapter because little is known about possible genetic factors in crime. It is known that the average IQ of prison populations is lower than the average IQ of people who have never been in prison. Moreover, the children of criminals tend to break the law more frequently than do children of law-abiding citizens. Some writers regard these facts as evidence for the inheritance of criminality, that criminals are caused by "bad seed." There is an old idea that there is a criminal type of face and body that may be recognized by experts, but when these "experts" are tested for their ability to identify bad guys and good guys, they cannot do it.

At the beginning of this book I said that when one event follows another, it does not prove that the first event caused the second. Also, the association of two things or events does not prove that a causal connection exists between them. The lower-than-average IQ of prison populations may be due to the fact that stupid criminals are more likely to get caught than are smart criminals. And when the smart criminal gets caught, he is more likely to have a good lawyer who can help him beat the rap. It has been shown over and over that when people from the middle and upper classes are charged with crimes, they are much more likely to escape prison terms through the dropping of charges, acquittal, suspended sentence, or parole than are people from the slums.

There are two general classes of criminals who are seldom arrested and convicted. First, there are the members of organized crime who operate outside the law with good legal advice and protection by bribery. Second, there are the white-collar criminals who commit graft, fraud, embezzlement, and exploitation. They are generally skillful at avoiding detection, but if charged with a crime they have expert legal advice.

When prisoners and noncriminals of the same socioeconomic background are compared, there is little difference in their average IQs. It does seem, however, that people of low intelligence are more likely to turn to crime as a means of getting a share of the riches around them than people of average or high intelligence are. They are also less likely to get or hold jobs. If they live in a slum environment, they are more likely to commit simple robbery and crimes of violence. The incidence of crime is high in the slums.

I mention a faulty argument. Denmark is said to sterilize those who are genetically unfit for parenthood. Denmark has relatively little crime. It is concluded that the sterilization program is responsible for preventing crime in Denmark. And that this is evidence that criminality is inherited. The fact is that Denmark does not have a large-scale sterilization program. Only a few are sterilized each year for medical reasons. The percentage differs little from that of the United States so this cannot be the reason for less crime in Denmark.

During the past few years there have been a number of newspaper and magazine articles about inborn chromosomal defects that are supposed to predispose the bearer to crime. The so-called "X" and "Y" chromosomes determine whether a person's sex will be male or female. A normal female has two X chromosomes, and a normal male has one X and one Y chromosome. As mentioned previously, Down's syndrome is caused by an extra chromosome at position twenty-one. Similarly, an extra sex chromosome, either X or Y, tends to be associated with abnormal behavior. It is claimed that although about 0.2 percent of males have an extra X chromosome, the XXY abnormality occurs more than twenty times as often among the inmates of criminal and mental institutions as among males outside such institutions. The XYY abnormality is said to occur more frequently in violent criminals than among noncriminals. Men who bear the XYY abnormality are much more likely to be unusually tall and aggressive. However, only a small percentage of violent criminals bear one or more extra chromosomes. Some XYY individuals become solid citizens. Further research must be done before the effects of an extra one or two sex chromosomes on behavior is understood.

By implying that the causes of crime are probably environmental, I do not endorse the idea that the criminal is morally innocent because society has caused him to do wrong. This is an idea based on an interpretation of the relationship between the environment and the person with which I cannot agree. Man is responsible for his behavior. I do think, however, that the actions society takes against the criminal should be for the protection of society and for reform of the criminal rather than for revenge. Some forms of punishment are useful in motivating him to reform, but others turn him further against society. Some leading psychologists claim that rewards for good behavior are more effective than punishment for bad behavior. The United States has become one of the most crime-ridden nations in the world. It seems probable to me that the idea that the criminal is a morally innocent victim of society is one indirect cause of the rise in crime. Many social reformers, lawyers, judges, and religious leaders have accepted this belief and have placed the interests of the criminal above the rights of society. It seems to me that this belief is just as wrong as the belief that criminals are born that way.

A less controversial and more materialistic cause of the rise of crime is that crime pays and risks of conviction are small. In New York City, for example, the chances of going to prison for committing a felony are less than one in two hundred.

This country is spending about 5 billion dollars per year on its federal, state, and local police. When you add to this the costs of private protection, the courts, prisons, the loss of property, injury, and the loss of the productivity of the criminal, the total cost of crime in this country is estimated at more than 40 billion dollars per year.

Should criminals be encouraged to remain childless? I am in favor of this idea. Even though there is no convincing evidence that criminality has a genetic basis, the child of the habitual criminal is more likely to be born into an environment that encourages crime. It has been argued that each habitual criminal should be sterilized. I am opposed to forcing any individual to submit to a surgical procedure. However, the procedures for sterilization of both men and women are simple and safe, and many habitual criminals might voluntarily seek sterilization if encouraged to do so. Some, perhaps many, do not want children and might welcome being able to copulate without risk of parenthood. At least some of them do not wish to pass their way of life on to a child. It seems to me that prisoners should be allowed normal sex lives—it is permitted in some countries—if they remain childless.

Our entire system of crime detection, detention, prosecution, judgment, imprisonment, and rehabilitation needs careful study and a revolution of methods. Most of our jails and prisons are horrible places, themselves schools for crime. I doubt that it will become possible to reform most habitual criminals. The answer lies in the prevention of crime by removing the environmental causes. And I suggest that encouraging habitual criminals to remain childless is one means of preventing crime.

Much of our lives is concerned with the defining and protection of human rights. Wars and crime take much of the attention of our governments and much of our national wealth. Most laws are made to prevent individuals and groups from taking advantage of other individuals and groups. Our other great concerns are for health and competence. Alexander Pope put it all into the following verse:

Know, all the good that individuals find,
Or God and Nature means to mere Mankind,
Reason's whole pleasure, all the joys of Sense,
Lie in three words—Health, Peace, and Competence.

VII

Aggression and War

This will be another short chapter for it also concerns crime, but on a more global scale, the crime of war. We really do not know that the personality trait of being aggressive has very much to do with the making of war. To be thought aggressive or nonaggressive is usually a judgment based on the behavior of an individual toward other individuals. The leaders of nations who make war are not commonly the hot-tempered type who are inclined to sock a rival in the nose. They are usually far removed from the action and are not inclined to get close to it.

Quite a bit is known about the inheritance of aggressiveness in the lower animals. It is possible to breed bulls, dogs, chickens, rats, and fish that are aggressive and will fight to the death. It seems probable that any species could be selectively bred for aggressiveness. I have even heard of aggressive rabbits.

There has been an interesting change in the belief of many behavioral scientists about aggression in animals. Most of us have been taught from childhood that many wild animals freely attack each other and especially man. And so we are afraid of lions, tigers, cougars, bears, wolves, and other animals. But nowadays it has become fashionable for behavioral scientists to claim that wild animals never attack unless they are hungry or are defending their territory, mates, or young. It is claimed that man is the only animal that will kill senselessly. It is true that wild animals usually retreat rather than attack. Stories about their being dangerous have been exaggerated. But some professors of the idea that man is the only wanton killer have led sheltered lives. Naturalists who have spent much of their lives in the forests, jungles, and plains know that some individual animals in many species kill needlessly. For some, such as a cat worrying a mouse or a dog tormenting a sheep, it is a form of play. It is possible that senseless killing occurs about as frequently in a number of other species as it does in man. Most human beings avoid it when possible. But it is sad that man, with his superior brain and the civilization he has developed, has not eliminated war and violence from his way of life.

Man's nervous system, the brain especially, still includes those parts of it that have been involved in anger-aggression and fear-flight syndromes. These modes of behavior were important in the evolution of animals and man. They may be modified by stimulating certain parts of the brain with an electric current. Wires are inserted into the brain through tiny holes drilled in the skull and may be left there for long periods of time. Stimuli to certain parts of the brain cause the animal to attack; stimuli to other parts of the brain calm the animal and stop the attack. There are drugs that calm aggressive animals and others that excite them.

There are people whose brains have been damaged by

disease or by injury who have fits of rage and become violent and assaultive. With at least some of these patients, a brain surgeon can suppress or prevent aggressive behavior by removing parts of the brain, stimulating other areas electrically, or administering certain drugs. (See Suggested Readings, page 140, for V. H. Mark and F. R. Ervin, *Violence and the Brain*.) However, most aggression seems to be learned behavior and is not caused by damaged brains.

Some scientists and some science writers have been predicting that drugs, wires to the brain, and brain surgery will someday be widely used to control man's behavior and to abolish violence and wars. But it seems unlikely to me that there are any practical biological ways to abolish wars, mob actions, and aggression. It is more hopeful to think about the fact that the people of some countries have not been at war for a long time. Wars are usually made by national leaders who are more likely to act from a calm, calculating thirst for power than from blind rage. And when the leaders of a rival country react to threats from an aggressor, it is also likely to be a quiet state of apprehension rather than an emotional storm of panic and terror. Of course the general attitudes of ordinary citizens are important in the making of some wars. National, religious, and racial prejudices and hates may be widespread. If the people of a country do not already dislike the people of a rival nation, the national leaders may attempt to arouse hate by propaganda.

Our sex hormones affect aggressiveness. In general, males are more likely to fight than females. The aggressiveness of the male is decreased by castration. There is a well-known experiment on the peck order of chickens that illustrates the effect of the male sex hormone, testosterone. The rooster rules his flock, but there is a peck order among the hens. When any two hens disagree over such matters as food or position on the roost, they may fight a bit but one hen soon gives up. The entire flock of hens works out a peck order with dominant hens at the top and submissive hens at the bottom. In this experiment a poor old hen at the very bottom of the peck order was given testosterone, the hormone secreted by the testes of males of all vertebrates, including man. She then became aggressive and worked herself to the top of the peck order in the flock. Although most species do not have such a well-organized order of aggression-submission, there is a tendency for the male sex hormone to stimulate aggression.

At the present time, women are seeking equal rights with men. This has led to debates over the role of biological differences between men and women in drives and in job success. It is argued that women are not biologically and psychologically suited to serve as national leaders. Biological bases for some sex differences in behavior are real, but in my opinion the tendency of human females to love peace is a trait that would suit some women for national leadership. If there were a way to turn over all world leadership to our wisest women, I would be willing to have the experiment tried because of the hope that they might bring peace to the world.

VIII

Social Welfare

Our national concern for social welfare began in the 1930s during the Great Depression. Prior to that time, most welfare was taken care of at the local level and was supported by private charities and some local public funds. The poor sometimes begged for clothes, food, and shelter or went to church groups for help. Neighbors of the very poor would help them. In rural areas and small towns there were many generous neighbors. When people became old and helpless, their children either cared for them or they were taken to the local poor farm. These were generally miserable places.

Everyone was supposed to do his or her best to earn a living. In rural areas it was usually possible to eke out a living with a team, a plow, and a few acres of rented land. Some of the poor in cities were also self-employed, as by doing piecework in the home. Now the small farm has almost disappeared. The rural poor of the South no longer pick cotton for a living. There are many other changes that have caused people to move to the cities. Very few of the poor are now self-employed.

There has been an accompanying change in the social

conscience of many people. There is broader concern for all the poor, not just one's neighbors. Modern welfare programs are planned on the assumption that we can abolish poverty by education and by spending to bring all the poor into the middle class so that they and their children will become self-sufficient. Our politicians promise to bring power and a better life to the poor. Our modern social welfare programs prevent quite a lot of human misery, and they enable some people to escape a deprived environment. But the birthrate in the slums is high, and the number of welfare clients continues to grow. In my opinion there is not the slightest chance that presently existing programs will cure the common causes of poverty and incompetence.

There are also permanent pensioners such as the crippled, blind, and the aged. A high percentage of them will always be dependent upon society for social welfare.

Costs

The cost of welfare for about 13 million Americans amounted to about 14.2 billion dollars for the year 1970. The federal government pays about half the costs and state and local governments pay the rest. The federal government budgeted about 8.7 billion dollars for the year 1971 and found it necessary to increase this amount during the year. A total of 16.3 billion dollars was spent on welfare during the fiscal year ending June 30, 1970. At that time 14.3 million persons in the nation were receiving cash welfare payments. In 1972 the number was more than 15 million. It is estimated that aid is received by only about half the needy and eligible, and the amount of aid received is commonly too little.

The United States ranks fourteenth among the nations in infant mortality, seventh in the percentage of mothers who die in childbirth, eighteenth in life expectancy for males, eleventh in life expectancy for females, and sixteenth in death rate for middle-aged males. There are demands that spending for health and welfare be vastly increased. The Department of Health, Education, and Welfare has warned that the national costs for welfare may double again in five years if steps are not taken to reverse the trend. During 1970 there was an increase of more than a million Americans whose incomes fell below the poverty line.

President Nixon said during the National Governors Conference in 1969, "We confronted the fact that in the last five years the federal government alone has spent more than a quarter of a trillion dollars on social programs—over 250 billion. Yet far from solving our problems, these expenditures had reaped a harvest of dissatisfaction, frustration, and bitter division."

In New York City the number of people on welfare has increased from 328,000 in 1960 to more than a million in 1970 and is growing at a rate of about 60,000 per year. There is now an average of one person out of six on welfare, and the number may increase to 3 million out of a total population of 8 million according to an estimate by the New York City commissioner for social services.

The federal program of Aid to Families with Dependent Children (AFDC) serves a merciful purpose for more than 11 million individuals. The program was intended to be temporary, for it was imagined that the need for it would fade away as other aid programs developed. It grows and grows. Since most of the mothers in the program are unskilled, they cannot earn enough to pay the cost of child care and the cost of travel to and from jobs and have as much money left over as they can get from AFDC.

The problems of the aged are growing, too, for they are increasing in numbers. Even when people who live into retirement years have planned carefully for this period of life, inflation has often robbed them of the expected buying power of their savings, Social Security, and annuities. Although many children support and care for their aging parents, an increased number choose to ignore them.

There are two general reasons why the size of welfare programs continues to grow. First, these programs fail to remove the basic causes of dependency. Second, the activities of welfare workers have more to do with recruiting clients than with teaching them to become self-sufficient.

Some Causes of the Problems

People become dependent on welfare for many different reasons. Some are physically handicapped and others are aged. The majority of federal welfare clients are AFDC mothers and their children.

In 1932, I began working part-time for a research program at the University of Minnesota that was studying the causes of unemployment. After the program had been planned and funded, the Great Depression came and a lot of people lost their jobs although they were hardworking and competent. Many thousands of unemployed were tested by the psychologists in this program. They did interviews and gave intelligence tests and other tests of special skills and aptitudes. Those people who had a history of always being unemployed were commonly of low intelligence, and they lacked aptitudes for anything more than unskilled labor. A few of them were mentally ill.

It seems probable that many people who are unemployable are mentally retarded or mentally dull. The fact that many are early dropouts from school may be less important. There are people with little schooling who become skilled and semiskilled workers by on-the-job training. I am not saying that education is unimportant, but the lack of it does not mean that a person need stay "down and out."

There are large numbers of retardates who are never counted among the unemployed because they never seek jobs or unemployment compensation. They may be inmates of institutions for the mentally retarded, or they may live with their families and are kept more or less out of sight. Other individuals of good intelligence are out of work because they are ill, lack the drive to work, or have the wrong attitudes toward work and are repeatedly fired when they try a job. Others are victims of circumstance, such as many of the AFDC mothers whose husbands do not contribute to child support. And finally, during economic recessions or depressions, many highly qualified professional and nonprofessional workers lose their jobs through no fault of their own and find it necessary to seek relief.

There is something else going on today that seems cruel and unjustified to me. This is the increased tendency of large companies to fire their employees or to pressure them into early retirement as they get older. It is generally true that people slow down as they age. There are exceptions. Some people remain good workers long after reaching retirement age. Some welcome early retirement when their savings and retirement pensions provide enough money. Others face hardship when discharged before planned retirement. When an individual has worked long and effectively for a company and is suddenly cast aside, this is a great blow to his pride. It seems to me that as companies grow in size, some of them become more and more indifferent to the pride and welfare of loyal employees and do no more for them than is required by labor laws and union contracts. I would not be sorry to see industry pressured into giving job security to all loyal, efficient employees.

Dislike of school and jobs may be learned in early life and last throughout life. These attitudes may be a part of the cultural heritage in slums, and they are contagious. The rationalization that "the world owes me a living" may be learned and repeated, parrotlike, throughout life. But there are many causes of social dependency, and there are many different attitudes among welfare clients. It is not true that all of them are lazy and seek to avoid work. Neither is it true that all of them want to earn their way in life and would do so if given opportunities; some are "the chicks that peep but do not scratch."

Our national leaders and many social scientists have assumed that creating good housing, good schools, and fair employment practices will suffice to reduce social welfare to a minor problem. They have ignored the roles of cultural and biological inheritance.

Public housing programs have cleared away some slums as well as some sound buildings. Much public housing is high-rise and is not liked by the people living in it. Some public housing less than fifteen years old has been wrecked and abandoned. In some areas thousands of apartments remain empty because of the great amount of crime in the area. I have already commented on the failure of increased spending to change the outcomes of education (Chapter V).

Costly programs of training the unemployed have had minimal success. Many business concerns have been pressured into hiring and training the hard-core unemployed, frequently at the expense of replacing reliable, competent employees. Despite newspaper stories that a high percentage of hard-core problem cases become better-than-average workers, I have not been able to confirm this claim in talks with the personnel managers of some of the companies that have hired such workers. They recite tales of woe instead.

THE FUTURE

It seems to me that a substantial percentage of steady welfare clients should not have children. Counseling of the socially dependent should be done by a newly created professional class of counselors who would work closely with physicians trained to do genetic counseling. Advice should be given after careful study of each client, not merely on the basis of he or she receiving welfare aid or being a so-called "dull normal" according to intelligence tests.

To be born into a culture that enslaves may be as much of a handicap to a child as to be born with defective genes. It is common for family histories to show parents, children, and grandchildren on welfare rolls. Some are there because they inherit low intelligence and possibly low drives. Some have poor health. Others come onto welfare and stay there because they have inherited a culture that does not respect education, job responsibility, the property of others, the law, and the rules of society. These social ills are just as contagious as some physical ills and should be quarantined to prevent spreading. The drawing of analogies does not prove a point, but it seems to me that placing children of harmful culture with children of enriched culture in order to correct the effects of the harmful culture does not work any better than trying to cure smallpox by putting its victims among well people. The outcome is to spread both kinds of disease—biological and social—to well people. On the other hand, I do not suggest returning to the old ways of isolating the sick and poor and then forgetting them.

A second means of attacking the problem is to develop intensive child-care and youth programs that keep the child busy at useful activities, including sports, during the waking hours. The development of day-care centers for the children of working mothers is a step in this direction. Unfortunately, in many instances the quality of these programs and the quality of supervision are poor. The professional competence of the people who conduct these programs should not be less than that of good schoolteachers. Indeed, these programs should aim at education rather than at mere custodial care.

The overall aim of all welfare programs should be to prevent the development of social dependency. No cures exist.

IX

Birth Control

Many parts of the Earth are overpopulated. Most authorities agree that the population growth of the United States must be slowed down. This means that the average size of the family must be reduced by the practice of birth control. I agree with this and make the added recommendation that there should be a selective practice of birth control so that the only children born are those who are wanted and have a reasonable chance to be healthy, self-sufficient, good citizens.

The Problem

No species can breed freely for a long time without reaching overpopulation. The usual checks on human population growth are starvation, disease, and wars. There is another check on the population growth of some species of animals—fertility is decreased by severe overcrowding. However, this is not known to be an effective check on the growth of human populations.

The Earth has about 3.8 billion people, and the number is increasing by about 70 million per year. The total population is expected to double by the end of this century—that is, to reach about 7 billion people. About 85 percent of this increase is expected to occur in the countries least able to feed their people. The United States alone now has more than 200 million people. Although there has been some recent decline in birth rate (the average is approaching two children per family), we have a large number of young people who have grown up from the baby boom of World War II. They have reached the reproductive age, so it is expected that our population of new babies will increase rapidly in the next few years. Children already born may double our college enrollment—now at 6 million—within the next ten years.

Some radical thinkers claim that if we were to raise all the food that is technically possible, the Earth could support more than fifty billion people. This is just a theoretical possibility. Man seldom does things efficiently. How would the increased pollution be handled? We are already in serious trouble with pollution and about two-thirds of the people on Earth are undernourished. However, I also believe that those scientists are wrong who predict an early doom for the United States, such as famines by 1975 and so much pollution of land, water, and air that by the year 2000 Earth will not support human life. Man can partially adapt to most poisons. But these problems are serious, and they worsen as man increases his numbers.

Uncontrolled population growth may possibly lead to the use of nuclear weapons. It is sometimes said that the bomb is the solution to our population problems. This is a horrible idea. Should anything human be left after nuclear warfare, it is unlikely to survive exposure to the radioactivity remaining after the explosions end.

Some authorities say that population growth must be reduced to zero; that is, there should be no more births per year than deaths. Others think that a slow rate of population growth is tolerable, and still others think that the population of the Earth should be decreased.

If every woman had but two children, this would not maintain the population indefinitely; it would slowly decrease. Why? Because not all children live to become adults and not all adults have children. Taking present vital statistics as a basis for calculations, it is estimated that the average family should be about 2.11 children in order to balance births and deaths. (Of course no one has a fraction of a child; I am referring to a statistical average.) However, after an average of 2.11 children per couple were achieved, it would take many years before the population stopped increasing in size. This would be so because the population has grown rapidly—many more people have been born than died—in recent years, especially during and following World War II. Many babies exist who will have children and live many years before they begin dying of old age. In other words, if a population has been growing rapidly, many years are required for it to balance births and deaths after it begins to make the attempt. Many people who write and talk about this problem imagine that if everyone began limiting family size tomorrow, the growth of population would stop immediately.

The only human way to limit population size is by birth control. (See Suggested Readings, page 140, for book by Garrett Hardin.) It has been estimated that in the United States about 85 percent of educated women practice birth control, whereas only 10 percent of uneducated women practice it. This would seem to provide a simple answer to why our welfare problems are rapidly increasing: the uneducated people are outbreeding those who are educated. Nevertheless, although women below the poverty line tend to have large families, a smaller-than-average number of them do have families. I am not sure that this is true in all parts of the country and among all ethnic groups; but the question of whether people below the poverty line are outbreeding those above the poverty line clearly still needs further study.

METHODS OF BIRTH CONTROL

The simplest way of preventing pregnancy is to avoid sexual intercourse, but since intercourse is a source of enjoyment and release from sexual tensions, it does not do any good to tell people not to copulate.

Another simple but not very reliable method of birth control is the rhythm method. The average sexually mature woman ovulates once every twenty-eight days, although the length of the period varies somewhat. The egg cell is discharged and begins working its way down the fallopian tube on about the fourteenth day after menstruation began. In order to avoid fertilization of the egg cell, a woman should abstain from having sexual intercourse for about four days before ovulation and for about three days afterwards. One reason for not copulating for a few days before ovulation is that the sperm cells may stay alive for a day or two. Counting the day of ovulation, this makes eight days in all. Since most couples do not have intercourse during menstruation, this makes about fourteen days of the "safe" period.

After the egg cell is discharged, it stays in the fallopian tube for a few days before it is destroyed. One reason why this method is not very reliable is that the time of ovulation varies in relationship to the beginning of menstruation. There are better ways of telling when it occurs than by the calendar, such as by recording a change in body temperature. The long and short of it is that many women who use only the rhythm method become pregnant.

Another simple means of birth control is *coitus interruptus*. (Coitus is a Latin word for copulation and *interruptus* is a Latin word meaning to interrupt.) It means to withdraw the penis from the vagina just before ejaculation. This requires more self-control than most couples have. Even when they intend to practice it regularly, they are likely to get careless. There is also always the risk that a little semen with some sperm cells will be discharged before the orgasm takes place.

The condom is widely used to prevent pregnancy. This is a rubber or plastic sheath that covers the penis. The name "condom" is supposed to come from its inventor, one Dr. Conton. Because some states have laws prohibiting the sale of birth-control devices, condoms are frequently sold as prophylactics, meaning that their purpose is to prevent disease. Not all are made of good materials, and they sometimes leak or break. It is a common practice to blow them up with air and inspect them for leaks upon purchase. Another objection to them is that they decrease the pleasure of sexual intercourse by preventing direct contact between the penis and vagina.

For several centuries it was a common practice to insert some preparation into the vagina prior to intercourse; this was supposed to kill the sperm cells after ejaculation. There were all sorts of home recipes for this preparation, none very effective and a few harmful. There was a related practice of douching out the vagina after sexual intercourse and adding some agent like vinegar to the water that was supposed to kill the sperm cells.

Putting some sort of mechanical barrier across the cervix (mouth) of the uterus has been used for a long time. Two types of devices have been common. One was a pessary with some sort of stems inserted into the uterus and leaving a button covering the opening. These were sometimes made of gold. Metal pessaries tended to cause infections and mechanical injury to the uterus and vagina, and they had to be removed before menstruation each month. They are no longer used. The second device was a rubber diaphragm, also called a pessary, that was inserted into the vagina to cover the mouth of the uterus before sexual intercourse.

The pharmaceutical industry has also developed creams, foams, and jellies containing chemical agents that destroy sperm cells but do not harm the vagina. Most doctors recommend that a rubber diaphragm be used that is coated with the foam, cream, or jelly before its insertion into the vagina. Women are taught how to insert the diaphragm so as to cover the cervix of the uterus. More of the foam, cream, or jelly is then injected into the vagina. It is removed and followed by a douche several hours after sexual intercourse. When properly used, this is a reliable method, although the diaphragm is sometimes displaced during intercourse, causing some failures. One objection to the method is that it is a bother to prepare and insert the diaphragm prior to intercourse.

It is an old practice of some peoples to put foreign objects into the uterus of domesticated animals to prevent pregnancy. In recent years little plastic coils (other shapes are used, too) have been developed that can be placed inside the uterus of a woman. These are called *intrauterine devices* (IUDs). The device may be left there for months and months to prevent pregnancy. No one knows just why this works. It does not stop ovulation and it does not stop the movement of sperm cells up the uterus. However, it does prevent the growth of an embryo from getting started. It is quite reliable and seldom causes any harm. Once in a while an IUD may irritate the uterus, penetrate the wall, or it may get expelled from the uterus. There is hope that IUDs may be made completely reliable and harmless for all users.

Finally there is "The Pill." About forty years ago, it was discovered that the administration of two sex hormones of the female, estrogen and progesterone—each produced in the ovary—would inhibit ovulation in laboratory animals. During the next few years, a great deal was learned about how this works. One of the leaders in this research was Gregory Pincus. He was influenced by Margaret Sanger to try to develop a simple means of birth control for women. You may know that Mrs. Sanger was a nurse who started the birth-control movement in America in the early part of this century. She was a wise, determined lady who had more than any other person to do with changing the attitudes of the public and our national leaders about the need for birth control. There was widespread opposition to it for a long time.

Gregory Pincus was a biologist who studied reproduction and the actions of sex hormones in laboratory animals. With the help of other biologists and a prominent physician, Dr. John Rock of Boston, he set about to make a preparation of hormones that could be taken by mouth and that was almost 100 percent effective in preventing pregnancy. Other scientists then developed pills which prevent ovulation. These pills are now widely used as a method of birth control in America.

Two or three years ago there was a hubbub in the newspapers, magazines, and television about claims that pills were dangerous. Experiments on animals had given some reason to expect trouble from receiving large amounts of the sex hormones over long periods of time. Actually, very little trouble has developed. The amounts of hormones in birth-control pills are probably not large enough to cause much trouble. A few women taking them get clots in their blood vessels; this also occurs in women not taking them, but a little less frequently. However, a higher percentage of pregnant women get clots in blood vessels, so it seems safer to be taking the pills than to be pregnant. These sex hormones had been used in human medicine for a number of years before the birth-control pill was put on the market. It seems to be among the least harmful preparations of drugs; the chemicals used in it have biological activities identical with those of the hormones produced in the body.

It seems probable that new methods now being tested will make it possible to prevent ovulation for months at a time by a single injection of a hormone preparation. It may also become possible to prevent pregnancy in a woman for a long time by implanting a pellet of a long-acting drug under the skin.

Although there are substances that interfere with the production of sperm cells in men, those presently available are harmful. It may become possible to sterilize men with drugs, but it is much more simple to make birth-control drugs for women. She is host to the whole process of fertilization of the egg cell, its movement down the tubes, and its attachment to the wall of the uterus.

There are therefore several points at which it is possible to interfere with the beginning of pregnancy.

Methods of Sterilization

The removal of the testicles of the male and the removal of the ovaries of the female are obvious means of preventing the production of sperm and egg cells. In the male this is called *castration*. It is also proper to speak of castration of the female, but removal of the ovaries is usually called an *ovariectomy* or *oophorectomy*. Castration is no longer used to sterilize human beings because there are much easier methods and because it takes away the sex hormones secreted by the testes and the ovaries.

The most simple way of sterilizing a man is to cut and tie the cut ends of the tube, or duct, that carries the sperm cells from the testicles. This duct is called the *vas deferens* and the operation is called a *vasectomy*. The operation can be done in a doctor's office under a local anesthetic; it is very simple and causes little discomfort. Not every doctor knows how to do the operation, however, so it should be done by a surgeon who has adequate training and practice. Contrary to common fears, a vasectomy does not affect the secretion of hormones by the testicles, and it does not decrease the sex drive or the pleasure of sexual intercourse. The number of men who have had a vasectomy has increased dramatically during the past year or two. Several hundred thousand per year have volunteered for the operation. If a woman copulates only with a sterile male, then she has no need for other methods of birth control.

The comparable operation in women is to cut and tie the cut ends of the two fallopian tubes so that egg cells cannot reach the uterus or be fertilized by sperm. This operation is called a *tubectomy*. It is more difficult than a vasectomy because the ovaries and tubes are inside the abdomen. The usual procedure is to cut through the skin and muscles of the abdomen, but the operation may also be done by going through the vagina and reaching the tubes without having to go through the belly wall and make a scar. This is a more difficult approach. Sometimes when a woman is having surgery that requires opening the lower abdomen, such as a Caesarean birth, she arranges with the surgeon to tie off her tubes.

ABORTION

Abortion means to cause an embryo or a fetus (an older embryo) to be expelled from the uterus so that it does not survive. It sometimes occurs spontaneously. When this happens very early in the life of an embryo, the mother may not be aware that an embryo has been reabsorbed or discharged from the uterus. When it happens several months later, it is called a *miscarriage*.

It is a very old practice to end an unwanted pregnancy by inducing an abortion. It is a dangerous practice unless done by a qualified physician. The general methods used illegally have been to injure the embryo in some way or to give a drug that causes the uterus to contract violently. When done by a person with some knowledge of surgery, the general method is to insert instruments through the vagina and mouth of the uterus and scrape out the contents of the uterus. This procedure is called a *curettage*. There are also new procedures for aborting an embryo. It can be removed from the uterus by suction, and new drugs are being tested that cause the embryo to be reabsorbed after it begins to grow.

Induced abortion has been considered a form of murder and is illegal in many parts of the world. And yet it has been practiced extensively. It is claimed that about a million abortions are done in the United States each year, but this may not be be a reliable estimate. The practice, however, is increasing. It is generally a step taken in desperation by a pregnant woman—many are married—who does not want to bear a child. Since abortion has usually been practiced outside the law by untrained people, there is grave risk of infection, extensive bleeding, too much anesthetic, injury to the uterus, and death. Abortion has now been legalized in a few states. When done by a trained physician under hospital conditions, the procedure is simple and safe. The risk is much less than that or normal childbirth.

In summary, the practical methods of birth control include the birth-control pill; plastic IUDs placed in the uterus; use of the diaphragm together with foams, creams, or jellies that kill sperm; sterilization; and induced abortion. I will discuss the ethics of these methods in a later chapter.

X

Selective Population Control

I believe that population growth must be controlled. Most people agree on this point. I do not agree, however, with the popular notion that all people are equally qualified to have children. I believe that some should remain childless. In this book I have attempted to describe how those who are unqualified for parenthood contribute to some of our great social problems. I do not believe that our population problems can be solved by merely encouraging each couple to have two children and then stop, or that competent, responsible people should have no children of their own but should adopt children from the large families of the underprivileged instead.

In this chapter I am going to be more specific about how we might develop a program of selective population control. Who are the people who should be encouraged to remain childless and who are the people who should be encouraged to have several children per family? How can we motivate individuals to cooperate without using forcible methods?

HEALTH

Several hundred diseases are known to be caused by simple genetic defects, and there may be genetic factors among the causes of almost all diseases. Most diseases caused entirely by known genetic defects are rare and these defects are usually recessive. I believe that everyone should be taught the general facts about the inheritance of disease and should be encouraged to seek genetic counseling from physicians trained in this speciality when they are concerned about their fitness for parenthood. At the present time there are too few physicians trained in this field. It is sound practice for a physician to explain any possible risks to a couple, express his judgment on whether or not they should have a child, but leave the final decision to the couple.

As people become more tolerant of artificial insemination, there will be increased use of it. When a husband is sterile or is a known carrier of defective genes, a couple may decide that the wife should receive sperm from a healthy donor. It may also become possible for a wife who is a known carrier of genetic defects to have a fertilized egg cell from another woman implanted in her uterus. If the breakdown of the institution of marriage continues, more and more women may choose to have artificial insemination when they wish to become pregnant and will copulate only for pleasure. They will have the opportunity to have children fathered by healthy, competent sperm donors.

It is becoming possible to detect more and more defects in the embryo during early pregnancy. A mother may then choose to have the embryo aborted rather than give birth to a defective child. A number of individuals would probably choose to remain childless if the risk of having defective or ill children was judged to be high by their genetic counselor.

A conservative program of genetic counseling and voluntary choice, such as I recommend, would not significantly reduce the number of sick people for several generations. It would never do so unless the program were expanded as knowledge and experience were gained. It is especially important to improve the detection of carriers of recessive defects. The important point is to get a program started. If most people come to understand that the aim is to reduce human misery, it could grow into an effective program of preventive medicine.

There may be other developments that will enable medical scientists to repair or replace defective genes or prevent the defects they now cause. As I have said earlier, I am not hopeful that such developments will come as soon as some science writers predict. However, medical science can guide selective birth control by natural methods already available. Much of the knowledge needed to expand programs of selective population control may be gained by the experiences of medical and social scientists with small programs.

INTELLIGENCE

There are several million people in the United States who have an IQ of seventy or less. Many of them are childless, but those who mate become parents of about half of the mentally retarded born in the United States. Very few retardates are able to earn a comfortable living, provide a good home, or otherwise be good parents. Should not every effort be made to identify them and encourage them to remain childless? As a means of getting their cooperation, I would propose that they be paid to accept either sterilization or some other effective means of birth control. But laws requiring the sterilization of retardates could not be enforced. It is a very serious matter to force surgery on any person, and I am among those who are opposed to it.

How about people who are not retardates but who are mentally dull? Should they be encouraged to remain childless? It seems to me that the answer is yes for most of them. I do not suggest that judgments be made solely on the basis of a low IQ, but if the person has failed in school, is not self-sufficient, and is unable to maintain a good home, it is unlikely that he or she is qualified for parenthood. It seems to me that there would be no risk to the genetic and social competence of our population in encouraging retardates and the mentally dull to remain childless.

On the other hand, there might be some risk in encouraging only brilliant people to have larger-than-average families. Many people of average intelligence have qualities that we need in families, neighbors, and citizens. Of course we need some people of genius, too. It is too bad when a very gifted person who is healthy in mind and body fails to pass his or her exceptional genes on to future generations. However, I am reminded that some very brilliant parents have unhappy children.

Welfare Clients

Some people who are on welfare much of their lives, even some who are not very intelligent, are good parents, maintaining happy homes and successfuly teaching their children to become good, self-sufficient citizens who escape the slums. These are exceptions. Other families stay on welfare generation after generation, never having a good home, getting into trouble with the law, dropping out of school, and commonly becoming antisocial. Because of poor sanitation, poor nutrition, and poor health habits, slum dwellers tend to have many health problems. Even when they are of average or above-average intelligence, an unfavorable cultural inheritance may bring environmental enslavement when a child learns all the injurious habits and attitudes of his parents. Such parents are just as unqualified for parenthood as the retardates. Within these groups are parents who batter their children, fight a good deal, become alcoholics, drug addicts, and so on. In many instances the father fails to provide support for the mother and children. In New York City more than 60 percent of illegitimate babies are born to women on welfare rolls. Many such births are unwanted by the mother; they occur because, frequently being very young, she does not know how to avoid pregnancy.

Although many people on relief are intelligent and have no more than the average number of inherited diseases, the majority of steady welfare clients are below average intelligence and have a greater-than-average number of inherited diseases. If the majority of welfare clients could be encouraged to remain childless, we would make progress toward improving the genetic endowment of the average child. Welfare clients should be given the knowledge and services needed to practice birth control and should have access to free abortions to avoid bearing an unwanted child. In addition, I recommend that free sterilization should be available to all those who seek it. I recommend paying most welfare clients to remain childless but not otherwise forcing it.

These recommendations are not made with the idea that they can replace efforts to build good environments for the underprivileged. We need both the biological and the environmental approach to preventing social problems.

OTHER GROUPS

It seems to me that at least some classes of criminals, drug addicts, and alcoholics should remain childless. Even though there is not much evidence that a tendency to crime is inherited, the environment of most criminals is harmful to children. The same is true of the environments of those who are chronic alcoholics and those who are addicted to hard drugs.

Some healthy, intelligent people who live in middle- and upper-class socio-economic groups are poor parents. They have no more right to parenthood than do others who create human misery. What should be done about them? I do not know. This is a question for all of us to think about.

DISCUSSION

If a national program of selective population control were directed toward all individuals who for either genetic or cultural reasons are unqualified for parenthood, it would involve many millions of people. I do not imagine that all of them could be persuaded to remain childless. If the programs affected only half of them—I am guessing about the possible number—it could significantly limit population growth. If we could encourage people of good biological and cultural heredity to carry the greatest part of the reproduction load, this would be an important move away from a welfare state.

Plans to control population growth must focus on women to a greater extent than on men. There are two general reasons. First, it is easier to control the fertility of women—there are more simple, effective methods—than it is to control the fertility of men. Second, a woman may copulate with a number of male partners, and it is unlikely that all of them will have been sterilized or will use a condom. These are about the only means a man has to prevent the introduction of live sperm into the vagina during copulation. A number of males who copulate with many partners either couldn't care less if some of their partners become pregnant or may even boast of it without any feeling of responsibility to the mother or child. In many instances it is necessary for the woman to assume the responsibility for avoiding an unwanted pregnancy. It is not fair to women, but these are among the facts of life.

Sterilization of the husband is a useful means of limiting family size for many married couples when the wife copulates only with her husband. This has become the method of choice for many married men who do not wish to father more children. However, it is little used by men who are poorly qualified to be fathers.

It has been proposed that income tax laws be changed so that the tax deduction for a child would be decreased for each additional child. The plan would be unfair to those couples who should have larger-than-average families. It might encourage some wage earners to limit family size but would not influence those on welfare who do not pay an income tax. Some of them are motivated to have additional children in order to increase the size of their welfare check. I do not suggest that welfare aid to unemployed mothers be stopped. This would be inhumane. But it should be made more rewarding to such women to remain childless than to have children.

Perhaps a better system of rewards can be found than the direct payment of money. Some of the Communist countries guarantee everybody a job. However, in these and some non-Communist countries the jobs available to men and women of low competence are a miserable sort. You will find them sweeping the streets with a broom or enduring the stench of public toilets where they work as attendants. Jobs given the poor of low competence may have to be a simple sort but they should support the development of pride and dignity. It is now technically possible to eliminate most demeaning jobs.

Some authorities on population control do not believe that many people can be persuaded or coaxed into limiting family size. If competent, intelligent people respond to limiting and those who are incompetent and irresponsible do not, it is likely that the latter will outbreed the former. I find this possibility frightening, for I believe that irresponsibility tends to go along with low intelligence. But a number of social reformers do not worry about this at all. They suggest that people in the middle and upper classes stop having children and adopt the unwanted children from the slums. I am not opposed to the idea of couples in a good environment adopting children from a poor environment as a means of getting them away from it. But I do not favor the idea that the irresponsible be permitted to breed freely while those who are socially responsible are encouraged to stop having children in order to play foster parents to the children of the irresponsible.

I return to the prediction that it is going to be necessary to force people to limit family size. It has been proposed that each woman be sterilized after having two children. This would require forcing her to submit to surgery. A second proposal is that a very powerful anti-fertility agent be developed that could be added to the drinking water. We do not now know of any birth-control agent that can be diluted to this extent and still work. If there were such an agent, there would be risk of harmful effects, including the causing of birth defects, until it had been tested for years. A third plan is to implant pellets of antifertility agents under the skin of every woman of child-bearing age. A woman would have to apply for a license to have the pellet removed in order to become pregnant and have a child. The pellet would then be reimplanted. The method could be used to achieve selective population control.

Forcing birth control by any method would require that we live in a dictatorship or at least a much more highly regulated system. I am among those who already resent most moves that government makes to interfere in our private lives. It is argued that we are moving toward a dictatorship anyway and that if we do not stop population growth, we will face chaos and probably nuclear war. Before adopting forceful methods to achieve selective population control, I believe that we should try intensive education and material rewards to encourage cooperation. This would leave the final decision or sterilization, use of birth-control agents, and having a baby to the individual. I believe that these programs should be developed and administered by medical schools and other medical centers. Some programs of genetic counseling and birth-control already exist. Some receive federal funds but operate independently of bureaucratic control. Many medical centers are already involved in the development of community medicine which involve the establishing of satellite programs in outlying communities. I suggest that genetic counseling and birth-control clinics should be included in programs of community medicine. Federal funds but not bureaucratic controls are needed to subsidize these programs and provide rewards for some individuals to remain childless. Judgments on qualifications for parenthood would be made by physicians and a new class of social scientists trained to judge and to counsel.

How are we going to find out which plan of selective population control works best? The answer is to test each plan in a pilot study. In industry, when a new product is being developed or a manufacturing procedure is being changed, it is tried out on a small scale in a pilot plant. A pilot population-control project could be tested for relatively little money. Small but carefully planned pilot projects could be tested in different kinds of communities in our country. We could keep modifying a plan until it either yielded the best practical results or the whole idea fizzled out, forcing us to look for other solutions to the problem.

Among the criticisms of selective population control is the claim that we have to stop population growth right now and do not have time to fool around until we know more about genetic qualifications for parenthood and until we have carried out a series of pilot studies. It is said that we should immediately insist that no woman bear more than two children. We are not going to stop population growth overnight by any known means, and it should be just as easy and rapid to work toward selective population control as to continue breeding people who are enslaved by defective genes and by deprived culture.

Let us suppose that a plan of paying women to accept some effective means of birth control is being tested. One problem would be to determine the amount of money required and the method of payment required to achieve the objectives. Would the problem be spoiled by failures to cooperate and by attempts to cheat? Could all the legal problems be solved? These and many other questions could be answered by pilot studies.

Can our country afford to pay millions of people to remain childless? I believe it can afford to spend quite a bit to be relieved of the costs of wasted lives. What does society lose if a person is unable to earn a living and must be sustained by welfare? Accurate estimates cannot be made. Earnings and welfare costs vary from one place to another. If the person is a criminal, the losses to other people, the loss of property, the costs of crime detection, courts, jails, and prisons may become great. If a person needs medical and hospital care throughout life, this too costly. Let us make an estimate. Almost any unskilled but competent person can earn as much as $6000 per year. If such a person worked for forty-five years, his earnings would be $270,000. If the person is idle, work estimated to have this value is lost. Suppose that instead of earning a living, this person requires $3000 per year of welfare payments. This would add another $135,000 for forty-five years of life. This may be the wrong way to calculate the cost of a totally dependent person to society, but figure it any way you choose, it comes out to a frightening amount. But the most important cost is in misery and unhappiness. I believe society can afford to spend several thousand dollars to persuade each person who is unqualified for parenthood to remain childless.

The idea of guaranteed employment and the use of day-care centers could be tested in pilot projects. Day-care centers are not new and the number is growing, but they are frequently without professional supervisors. In the Soviet Union the women who run the child and youth programs have as much special training and are just as smart and responsible as are schoolteachers. We can learn a great deal about creating a healthy culture by studying the programs of countries such as the Soviet Union, Israel, England, Denmark, Switzerland, and others that have high literacy and relatively little crime.

I emphasize again that programs of social reform almost never work when put together in haste. When agencies of government—local, state, and federal—are under pressure to come up with instant solutions to a serious problem, they are likely to form committees, commissions, or task forces. The members meet and argue a lot and come up with a plan that is a compromise of most of the ideas among them. The first trial of the plan is likely to be full-scale. If a business tried to function this way, it would probably go broke. There is no real alternative to working slowly and cautiously if we are to make progress without wasting a lot of effort and money.

XI

The Ethics of
Selective Population Control

Society has ethical guides to the taking of a human life and now needs ethical guides to the giving of a human life.

The rules that guide man's conduct change according to the needs and fashions of the times. Many Americans have been guided by the words of Genesis, 9:1, "And God blessed Noah and his sons, and said unto them, 'Be fruitful, and multiply, and replenish the earth.'" Many take joy in having children and some take pride in having large families. When this country was young, it was important for each family to have several children earning an income, or if the family lived on a farm, all members were required to help with the work. Children were expected to support their parents during old age. Thus the morality and needs of earlier days encouraged large families. The parents of large families were considered to have been blessed by God.

When they mentioned it at all, most religions once taught that birth control was sinful. It was believed that the sole purpose of copulation was to beget children. Some states even passed laws against the sale of contraceptive devices and preparations. To this day, the Catholic Church forbids its members to practice any form of birth control other than the rhythm method. This is regarded as a natural way of avoiding pregnancy that does not require any artificial intervention with natural processes. However, many Catholics neither accept nor obey this dictum.

Some people have always believed it was harmful to most women to bear large numbers of children and that a woman should not conceive an unwanted child. The birth-control movement and family planning got started in the early part of this century in America, but many individuals and groups, especially religious groups, opposed the movement as interfering with the will of God.

When America was young and the population small, the threat of overpopulation was not apparent. More people were needed to build the country. Disease was an important check on population growth, then. Some of our national leaders thought of population growth as a means to military strength.

Until very recently it was generally taught and believed by religious groups and in many homes that each embryo is a person with a God-given soul or would become the temple of a soul at the time of birth. Induced abortion was regarded as a form of murder. All states passed laws prohibiting the practice of abortion unless it was necessary to save the life of the mother. Some states did not permit abortion under any circumstances. Attitudes, beliefs, customs, and laws are changing but this issue is still hotly debated.

The fact that population growth now threatens the future of civilization is an important factor in causing most people, including many Catholics, to agree that birth control is necessary and right. But arguments are still made against it. I will describe them and tell why I think that they are wrong.

BIRTH CONTROL

It has been claimed that man has no right to interfere with any of the processes of reproduction, for they represent God's will. One can believe in God without accepting this dogma. We interfere with nature and affect reproduction whenever we build a shelter, grow food, observe sanitation, or try to prevent and cure diseases. Does every living sperm cell and every egg cell have the right to a chance at union and to grow into a human being? Each woman produces an average of about four hundred egg cells during her lifetime. Is it God's will that each of these should become a baby? Almost all of these living cells waste away and die. Within a lifetime, each normal man produces several times as many sperm cells as there are people on earth. Should we weep because almost all of these tiny living, moving cells perish? About half of the eggs that are fertilized fail to become babies, for when something goes wrong the embryo may be destroyed in the womb by natural processes. Should we be sad because they do not survive to become sick or defective babies?

Human acts and decisions do influence the processes of reproduction. We have laws, religious guides, and social customs that discourage mating until a certain age is reached although boys and girls are capable of becoming parents before that time. We prohibit the marriage of close relatives. We try to keep prisoners and inmates of custodial institutions from copulating. The time of actual copulation is commonly determined by an emotional whim rather than a divinely guided intent to start a baby. Since man-made behavior and decisions influence each individual birth anyway, there does not seem to be any moral reason why man should not use his reason in family planning and to prevent overpopulation. Control of births helps protect the health of the mother, the child, and society. There are no reasons other than those given by religious dogma for thinking that God is trying to see that certain individuals get born and that man sins when he tries to interfere with a chance union of sperm and egg.

Another argument against the development of birth-control methods is that the availability of them encourages sexual intercourse outside of marriage. The fear of pregnancy is not a very effective way of preventing couples from copulating. Over 20 percent of first pregnancies occur outside of marriage. It seems probable that most of the children who are conceived out of wedlock are unwanted. Since people copulate outside of marriage despite the risk of pregnancy, shouldn't they be provided with a reliable means of preventing unwanted pregnancy? If these unions are sinful, why should any of the punishment be borne by the children, who are disadvantaged by being unwanted?

I have mentioned that birth control was once opposed by those who wished to encourage rapid population growth for economic reasons. This is no longer needed. Large families were also encouraged to provide soldiers when the size of armies was important in military conquest. The breeding of soldiers is no longer an aim of most civilized countries and individuals.

INDUCED ABORTION

Most people who are opposed to induced abortion claim that it is a form of murder. Some people have a religious belief that when a sperm cell and an egg cell unite, a soul comes into the embryo. Most scientists and more and more religious leaders believe that only the workings of nature are involved in conception, growth, and human life. However, quite a few people claim that each embryo is a tiny person and argue that the rights of the embryo should be recognized by the law and by society.

Professor Garrett Hardin has written a book on birth control and abortion to which I have referred before (see Suggested Readings). He has been a leader in educating the public about abortion, and his writings have persuaded me that it is not wrong for a pregnant woman to seek an abortion when she does not want to bear a child. He believes that the rights of the woman are greater than those of an unwanted embryo growing as a parasite in her body. He argues that an embryo is not a person but a biological blueprint of one that has the capacity to develop into a person. I prefer to call it just an embryo, not a blueprint. The embryo is much more like an unjoined sperm cell or egg cell than it is like a person. The same value may be attached to an embryo as to living egg and sperm cells, all of which are alive but can be wasted. Together with many biologists and physicians I do not regard an embryo as a person until it has a fully formed human body with a brain and becomes conscious of itself. Following development of the brain there is awareness, a will to live, and there can be a fear of death. These are some of the essential qualities of being human, and I would not destroy them.

I have been surprised to see how quickly public opinion has shifted from the view that an induced abortion is murder to the view that it is not murder and is not wrong. One factor in this change has been growing awareness that when an abortion is induced by a trained physician, it is much safer than having a baby. The idea that a woman has the right to decide whether or not she permits an embryo to grow in her body seems reasonable to many people. Those who oppose birth control and induced abortion say, "If you don't want a baby to grow in your body, don't copulate." This assumes that sexual intercourse is wrong unless it is done with the intent to conceive a child. Most of us regard it as a normal expression of the sexual urge and believe that it is ethical to separate it from parenthood.

Because induced abortion by trained physicians is safe and is becoming generally accepted, it may be used as a backup to ordinary methods of birth control. Since it is becoming possible to detect some genetic defects and some nongenetic defects in the early stages of pregnancy, it is likely that more and more defective embryos will be aborted rather than allowed to develop into handicapped children.

I have heard it argued that it is a rewarding, character-building experience to raise a seriously handicapped child. I am sure that a few parents find it so, but most of them dread it and some are crushed by it. Even in the first case, why should an avoidable but seriously handicapped child be brought into the world to benefit the parents? The aborted defective embryo may be replaced by a healthy one, perhaps by the same parents.

THE ETHICS OF CLONING

I have mentioned that it may become possible to reproduce man by cloning, that is, by replacing the nucleus of a fertilized egg cell with the nucleus of an ordinary cell of the body. The nucleus of the ordinary cell contains a full set of genes. The egg cell would then develop into an individual who would be genetically identical with the person from whom the ordinary cell was taken.

Does each person have the right to develop in the natural way? Does he have the right to be unique rather than a genetic copy of another person? This hypothetical individual can't exist unless he or she is cloned. Does a nonexistent person have rights? These are sticky confusing questions and they don't get us anywhere.

It is reasonable to argue that society has the right to aim for healthy, happy, wanted children and that in this respect it has rights over individuals, including medical scientists, who are trying to develop artificial means of reproduction. If we accept this principle, we may then argue that selective population control is ethical and that society may stop medical scientists from trying to grow babies by cloning if there is risk of harm to those grown from clones or to society.

In what ways could cloning be harmful? Cloned individuals might be born with defects. But suppose that they were just as healthy as the person from whom the cell nucleus was taken. A cloned person might be unhappy at being a genetic copy of another person, for he or she would be deprived of individuality. Such a person would not have the usual biological relationship to a father and mother. He would know that he came into the world by an artificial procedure. Cloning might grow into a widepsread program of artificial breeding. Perhaps a dictator would decide to clone a docile slave class of people. We may imagine all sorts of misuses of this and other artificial ways of breeding people, especially if governments got a hand in it. Many biologists and medical scientists are completely opposed to the idea of cloning man. They say it should not be done, not even once. Their objections are of the sort that I have just reviewed.

The idea of cloning does not appeal to me either. I see no reason to replace the natural processes of sexual reproduction. However, the possibility that cloning will be perfected and misused is not among my greatest worries about the future. In some parts of the world, if not in America, scientists will try to clone people. If it works, it is likely to be tried on a small scale, and its use may increase if there are no harmful outcomes. Future generations will make their own decisions as to whether it is useful or should be prohibited. It may not even work in man.

But I do agree that medical scientists and the public should look ahead and develop ethical guides to the use of knowledge. I have used cloning as an example of a possible future method of selective population control. I now return to the reality of the present.

SELECTIVE USE OF BIRTH CONTROL AND INDUCED ABORTION

I argue that reproduction should be limited to those persons judged capable of endowing children with a reasonable chance to achieve happiness, self-sufficiency, good health, and good citizenship. Many people do not agree with me. They believe that every person has an equal right to become a parent regardless of whether the children have a fair chance in life. I argue that individuals differ widely in qualifications for parenthood; there is evidence in abundance that this is so.

It is generally accepted that society has increased rights over the individual when society is in peril. In my opinion, population growth and the welfare state are each perilous. I argue that society has the right to establish controls over population growth and to shift the population load to the people who are best qualified for parenthood. These rights are greater than the rights of the individual to bring harm to society. Society must bring its numbers under control and should aim at each child having a good opportunity for health, happiness, and success.

Many individuals want to remain childless. This much is easy, for there are effective methods of birth control and of aborting unwanted pregnancies. Suppose that a couple plans to raise a family, but each of the parents has an inherited illness. Do they have the right to take the considerable risk that one or more of their children will become mentally ill? Also, their mental problems may make them poor parents. I believe they should be persuaded or coaxed into changing their minds. Other healthy, happy couples would like to have four or five children. They are good parents in all respects. Should not such couples have several children per family to make up for the couples who remain childless? Zero population growth is still possible for a nation.

A common question raised about selective population control is, "Who is going to decide about fitness for parenthood; who is going to play God?" This is a loaded question. It is an example of the logical fallacy called *plurium interrogationum,* or the fallacy of many questions. The question includes a false assumption. Nobody is going to play God, and it is foolish to imply that anybody could play God if he wanted to do so. Man chooses the events that lead to the union of an egg and sperm in the first place. Man will continue to play man. It is merely proposed that he do so intelligently. I repeat that the individuals who engage in genetic counseling should be physicians who are trained in this medical speciality. In addition, there should be professionals trained in the social sciences who advise on the social, economic, and behavioral fitness of the individual for parenthood.

Most of our guides to right and wrong represent fashions in thought. It seems possible that, after being informed about the issues, the public will agree that we should aim for happy, healthy, competent children and that child welfare has a higher ethical value than has the right to parenthood. Does any person have a natural right to bring a child in the world with an uncorrectable biological or environmental handicap to success? Some people, perhaps many, argue that society must cure its environmental problems and then no one will be born into a deprived environment or pass an environmental handicap on to a child. Few adults can rid themselves of antisocial ideas and attitudes that are learned very early in a substandard environment. It is doubtful that the availability of money and material changes in the environment can change the psychological nature of the adult. We must begin to train for citizenship during early childhood.

There is another important point about all efforts to influence human lives. There is always risk of mistakes and harm. No effort to benefit man works for everyone. Every medicine is harmful to a few patients. The best anesthetic agents and vaccines kill a few people and make others ill. There is some risk in all forms of surgery. We tolerate cars, planes, trains, and bicycles, but all of them lead to some deaths. The point is that everything we do involves risk for some people. We are inclined to accept risks when they are only possibilities, but we go to great lengths to protect the individual who is known to be in danger.

Programs of selective population control would involve risk of some mistakes. But I believe that we could shift the odds strongly in favor of child welfare, reduce much of today's misery, and strengthen that which is healthy in society.

Debates about right and wrong are influenced by the severity of a threat. In times of peril society is more inclined to place the rights of society above those of the individual. Thus, we are more likely to demand rights over individuals during war than during peace. The future of mankind is at stake now. The right of society to continue to exist and to become increasingly free of genetic and environmental handicaps seems more important than the right of an individual to act against the welfare of children and of society. Man determines his future whether he likes it or not. He should choose to determine it purposefully rather than blindly.

XII

Who Should Have Children ?

Advocates of family planning aim that every child should be a wanted child. Most of us agree that this is a good general aim. But it is wrong to assume that it always leads to happy, healthy children. Not every planned child turns out well and not every unplanned or unwanted child turns out badly. It is not unusual for a woman to be emotionally upset when she learns that she is pregnant, to fear and resent having a baby, and then to love it and be a good mother as soon as the baby is born. Other women plan each pregnancy very carefully, but when the baby is born, they let it interfere with their lives as little as possible. Some children are born into homes that could offer every environmental advantage but lack the most important conditions for a happy childhood, love and understanding. A great deal may be done in the home and in schools to teach the advantages of family planning and responsible parenthood.

I shall now describe some couples and individuals who need advice on having children. All these cases are fictitious, but the kinds of problems described are common.

Couple No. 1 seeks advice because the husband has epilepsy and both he and his wife have been told that the disease is inherited. Some forms of epilepsy have a genetic basis and others do not. On the basis of family history and neurological examination, it may be possible to judge whether the husband inherited a genetic basis for the disease. Unless both the husband and wife have a family history of epilepsy, the risk of a child's developing the disease would be very small. The counselor may be more concerned with psychological qualifications for parenthood. Is the epilepsy of the husband kept under control by medication? Is he steadily employed? Has the wife made a good adjustment to the disease of her husband? And has the husband made a good emotional adjustment to being an epileptic?

Couple No. 2 is in good physical health, and both have a family history of good health and longevity. They have a child that has been repeatedly beaten and injured by the husband. The wife has attempted to shield the husband by giving a false explanation of the injuries, but the hospital physicians are not deceived. The wife does not wish to have additional children. The husband rejects advice to seek psychiatric care but does agree to the proposal that he have a vasectomy done and that the child be placed with relatives.

Couple No. 3. Both the husband and the wife have been hospitalized with schizophrenia. They meet and marry while each is in remission. The husband has been hospitalized several times and the prognosis for lasting recovery is poor. Since there is good evidence that this disease is inherited and since neither of them is likely to be a comptent parent, they are encouraged to remain childless.

Couple No. 4. The husband and wife are both mentally

dull. The family of each has a history of general incompetence. They live on a tiny farm in a rural area where they barely manage to make a living. They have no knowledge of birth-control methods and receive no guidance. A large number of children are born to the couple, and three of them die in infancy. Two other children are retardates, and none is brighter than a dull normal. The overworked, poorly nourished wife ages rapidly and dies at the age of forty-one.

Couple No. 5 is also rural. Both are of average intelligence and have a family history of good health. Neither has continued formal education past high school. However, the husband has attended university short courses in agriculture, and each has learned modern methods of farming and home economics from clubs and the farm extension services of their state university. They study farm journals and take an active interest in local and state politics. They are industrious and make a modest profit at diversified farming. They have five healthy children who grow into industrious good citizens. This is an example of a couple who may be encouraged to have a larger-than-average family.

Couple No. 6. Each is a gifted musician and comes from a musical family. The wife wishes to bear a larger-than-average number of children in order to pass exceptional genes to future generations. There is risk that such parents will expect too much from their children, and they need counseling on this point. A child of such parents may or may not inherit musical talents and may or may not develop an interest in music. An ungifted child may feel rejected when it fails to fulfill the expectations of the parents. Gifted parents tend to have children who are, on the average, less gifted than they.

Individual No. 1 is an AFDC mother. She is of average

intelligence and has a family history of good health but is an alcoholic. She lives with a succession of male partners and moves frequently from one slum apartment to another. She gives birth to a baby every two or three years. Her income from welfare is sufficient to shelter and feed the children, but she sometimes leaves them alone for many hours. The children once narrowly escape a fire occurring in her absence. The culture into which her childern are born rejects education and embraces that of street gangs, where they learn the use of alcohol and drugs and the ways of violence at an early age. A daughter becomes pregnant at thirteen. A son is killed by a rival street gang. All the children learn to live outside the law and no member becomes a self-sufficient citizen. This woman would have preferred to be childless but had no opportunity to learn the methods of birth control.

Individual No. 2 is a successful young executive who does not become engaged to marry until he is past thirty years of age. During his engagement he develops a progressive neurological disease called Huntington's chorea. It is characterized by involuntary muscular movements, such as twisting and grimacing, and by mental deterioration. His betrothed is distressed but is willing to marry him immediately. The man would like to become a father but is advised that his disease is caused by a dominant gene; the chance that his child would develop the disease is fifty-fifty. He wisely and generously breaks off the engagement knowing that there is no likelihood that his disease can be cured and that his life expectancy is short.

Individual No. 3 is a young woman of above-average intelligence who is addicted to heroin. She supports her habit by prostitution. She has been treated for addiction several times, but the prognosis for a permanent cure is poor. During an unwanted pregnancy she seeks and obtains an illegal abortion. Had the pregnancy continued, the child would have been born addicted to heroin. She is encouraged to be sterilized and does have this operation performed. She does not live happily ever after, but she now avoids the risk of passing her environmental enslavement on to another generation.

Individual No. 4 is a habitual criminal who has served several prison terms. He has violated each of two paroles. He has never married but does not lack for sexual partners when he is out of prison. He prefers young unsophisticated girls and has impregnated at least a dozen of them. Some have ended their pregnancies by illegal abortion. None of those who have given birth to his children keeps the baby. Only one child has been adopted. The father neither assumes responsibility for his children nor for the mothers. He might accept free sterilization, but the possibility has never been suggested to him.

Individual No. 5 is a mentally retarded young man. His physical appearance is normal. He has been trained in a custodial school for retardates and is able to do simple jobs under close supervision. The court has appointed a relative as his legal guardian. He wishes to marry, but this plan is opposed by his guardian on the grounds that he will not be able to support a family. The dull normal girl who wishes to marry him is employed on a factory production line. If they remain childless, they are likely to be self-sufficient. If the girl should give up her job to raise a family, they will need welfare assistance and there is a risk that one or more children will be mentally retarded. There are retardates in each family. Neither of them is anxious to have a child, but no one guides them to methods of birth control or suggests sterilization. The girl takes the initiative to escape the guardian. They elope to a distant city, marry, and after a child is born they apply for welfare assistance.

I have given only simple examples of couples and individuals who need advice about parenthood. Many of these human problems are complex and can be handled wisely only when carefully studied by highly trained counselors. Everyone interested in social problems should visit the slums of our cities and rural areas, jails and prisons, the custodial institutions for retardates and the insane, the nursing homes for the aged, the hospitals that serve the poor, and finally the morgues of these hospitals. Much human sorrow is hidden in communities that the average citizen does not see, or it may be behind closed doors that are nearby.

To reject efforts to prevent these problems on the grounds that equal rights to parenthood is a basic freedom is far more radical and dangerous to freedom than are humane efforts to give children freedom from genetic and cultural enslavement. Again I quote from Tennyson:

> Chaos, Cosmos! Cosmos, Chaos! once
> again the sickening game;
> Freedom, free to slay herself, and dying
> while they shout her name.

XIII

Questions and Answers

In this chapter I have recorded some of the questions that have come to me after writing and lecturing on selective population control. I also provide my answers.

Question: I say that there is a difference between trying to persuade a person to do something good for himself and trying to persuade him to do something good for me that is harmful to him.

Answer: I agree. But persuading people who are not qualified for parenthood to remain childless may be good for them also, as well as for many individuals who make up society.

Question: Doesn't your proposal boil down to the recommendation that everyone who represents any kind of a problem in society should remain childless?

Answer: There are important environmental causes of most social problems, and some are caused almost entirely by a deficient environment. We must continue every effective effort to improve the environment. Some people who are problems in society are still qualified for parenthood.

Question: But you say that if an individual lives in a harmful environment this is reason enough to remain childless.

Answer: This is true unless the person is able to escape a harmful culture. It can be contagious and passed from one generation to the next. It is not commonly corrected by physical changes in housing and schools.

Question: Do you imply that it is useless to build good schools and housing for the underprivileged?

Answer: No, but these physical improvements alone do not correct all the problems of the underprivileged.

Question: What environmental changes would correct the effects of harmful culture?

Answer: I doubt that anything short of controlling the social environment during all waking hours of the child will do it.

Question: Wouldn't this require a dictatorship?

Answer: I am afraid so, but hope not.

Question: Why not work solely on improving the environment, including culture, rather than on trying to get people to stop having children?

Answer: We need to try both. Neither approach will be fully effective by itself.

Question: Give some examples of underprivileged individuals whom you regard as qualified for parenthood.

Answer: Within city slum and impoverished rural areas, there are couples of average or superior intelligence and a family history of good health who shelter their children from enslaving habits and attitudes. Their children are encouraged to do their best in school and to become industrious, responsible citizens. Some such families are often active members of a church. Religious education is frequently but not always helpful. Such families and especially the children have the chance to escape a poor environment.

Question: You seem to be arguing against yourself. If these families are smart and industrious, how did they get into the slums?

Answer: I have avoided generalizing about any socio-economic or ethnic group. There are different causes of poverty. Some people are poor because of misfortune, racial bias, and recent immigration or migration to escape some form of persecution. Just a few decades ago, many Jews and Asians lived in slums because they were not permitted to live elsewhere, and they were subjected to job discrimination. But each ethnic group had a home culture which encouraged education and hard work. Most Jews and Asians made their way out of the slums in spite of discrimination against them. There are still many individuals and families in slums who have the abilities and drives to work their way out. But others are there because they lack ability and drive or because they have a cultural heritage that destroys ambition and job responsibility.

Question: Why are you against poor people?

Answer: I am not against poor people; I am against the causes of poverty. One common cause of it is low intelligence, and a second common cause is a harmful culture.

Question: Isn't lack of opportunity a common cause of poverty?

Answer: Unequal opportunities are unfair, but most people are able to make their own opportunities when they are of average intelligence and are ambitious.

Question: Isn't the social inheritance of wealth, special privileges, and power a cause of poverty?

Answer: It is not fair for some people to inherit great advantages over others. To me, the ideal is to give everyone an equal start and equal opportunities in life, free from genetic and environmental handicaps. However, competent ambitious people who are not enslaved by bad culture are usually able to work their way out of poverty despite the existence of inherited wealth, special privileges, and power.

Question: How can the number of people on welfare be significantly reduced when most of them are children, the elderly, the ill and disabled, or welfare-supported mothers?

Answer: Responsible citizens do not bring children into the world until they can support them. Responsible citizens save money for old age and for periods of illness. I do not imply that all welfare needs could be abolished if only responsible, competent people bore children who in turn would have a good chance to become responsible, competent citizens. All of us risk unexpected misfortunes, and some more than others are handicapped by social injustices. But if the right to reproduce was limited to responsible, competent citizens, the welfare load and accompanying social malignancy could be steadily reduced.

Question: Do you reject the philosophy of communism?

Answer: Yes.

Question: Do you agree with the aims of some social reformers that everyone should receive good medical care and a minimal income?

Answer: Yes, but I think that every able individual should have to work for these benefits.

Question: Since many of the underprivileged are Negroes, isn't your proposal to encourage the underprivileged to remain childless a proposal for Negro genocide?

Answer: No. Let's examine the implications of your question. You seem to imply that according to the general guidelines I have described Negroes are not qualified to reproduce. In my opinion the great majority of Negroes—perhaps 75 percent—are qualified for parenthood. I am not sure about percentages for any ethnic group. Recent statistics show that Negro mothers in the middle and upper classes have an average of less than two children each. This is too few for these classes to reproduce themselves. According to the same set of statistics, Negro mothers below the poverty line have about four children each. The birth rate among Negro women on welfare is falling as they are offered information on birth control. If intelligence is an important factor determining success in life and if welfare mothers are outbreeding middle- and upper-class mothers, this is a grave threat to the future of Negroes. It means that in addition to all of their own problems, they may be drifting toward genetic enslavement. We cannot be sure just what is happening at present, but we should find out. One of the ways in which poor Negroes have been disadvantaged is that they have been deprived of information and services on birth control that are easily available to Negro and white women in middle and upper classes.

Question: Are you suggesting that different standards be applied to Negroes and whites in encouraging selective population control?

Answer: None whatever. But it is important for Negroes as well as whites to shift the burden of childbearing from the underprivileged to those best able to provide good homes for children.

Question: Suppose that an impoverished woman of any race was offered some sort of financial reward to remain childless but made the decision to have children. Would you be in favor of denying her support by AFDC?

Answer: No, it would not be humane to deny aid to the mother and her children. But I would try to make the rewards for remaining childless more attractive.

Question: Why would a woman in this position choose to have babies if she could easily avoid pregnancy?

Answer: A probable reason would be that she loved children and that having some of her own was the greatest satisfaction she could find in life.

Question: Could such a woman be encouraged to seek artificial insemination from superior sperm donors of her race and to copulate only for pleasure with other partners?

Answer: Maybe she should be given that choice.

Question: I've tried The Pill and it makes me nauseated. Why didn't you mention such effects?

Answer: It is true that some women develop reactions causing them to stop taking The Pill. But when the unfavorable effects are compared to the effects of dummy (placebo) pills during double-blind control studies, there are almost as many unfavorable responses to the dummy pills. Some women tend to gain weight while on The Pill. Whatever the cause of these effects, it is true that some women stop taking it because of unwanted symptoms.

Question: You said that vasectomy is very simple and then added that this operation should be done only by surgeons who are carefully trained in the technique. If it is so simple, why can't any doctor do it?

Answer: The day when most doctors did some simple surgery is past. Any surgery can be botched by a doctor who has not been trained as a surgeon. I will mention three risks in vasectomy. First, the surgeon may not correctly identify the *vas deferens* and may cut and tie something else. Second, sometimes there is an extra *vas deferens*, which the surgeon may fail to tie and cut. Third, if he fails to tie off the *vas deferens* properly, it may leak semen with sperm. If the semen gets into the blood stream through small, cut vessels the patient can develop an auto-immunity to his own cells. Such an error can be very serious. But there is no need for a patient to worry if he goes to a well-trained, experienced surgeon.

Question: You write very candidly about sexual intercourse and reproduction outside of marriage. Have you no respect for the sanctity of marriage?

Answer: I believe that married love that lasts the lives of the couple is much the best form of mating and is best for children. But I don't believe that marriages are made in heaven. I am being realistic by recognizing that a lot of people copulate outside of marriage and that a sperm cell can fertilize an egg just as easily outside of marriage. More than 10 percent of all babies are born out of wedlock and many more are conceived before marriage. Scolding people and calling them sinful is no longer effective. It is more useful to teach all people who copulate how to avoid having unwanted children.

Question: Do you regard the breakdown of the family as desirable?

Answer: No, but the trend may continue.

Question: You stated that recent studies have shown that Negro mothers below the poverty line have an average of about four children each. I have read a statement from the United States Social Service Department that the number of children per AFDC family was 2.8 in December, 1970. How do you explain this difference? Are Negro mothers with the largest families staying off AFDC?

Answer: Think carefully about the meaning of the

average that you quoted. Many of these mothers will have more children. Some began receiving AFDC as soon as they had their first child. The average of 2.8 children represents many partially completed families and the average of four children per family represents completed families. Also, the average total number of children per Negro mother below the poverty line is being reduced and may continue to decline.

Question: Is it not a greater wrong to destroy an embryo with all the promise of its future than to end the life of a badly deformed baby, a severe retardate, a hopelessly insane person, or one who is senile? There are many thousands of aged in nursing homes who are unwanted, unneeded, and unloved.

Answer: This is a painfully confusing question which I cannot answer to my own satisfaction. If the practice of abortion is used wisely, it will be reserved for those embryos that lack the promise of a good future. The embryo lacks a fully developed brain, it is not conscious of self, it has no will to live and no fear of death. The newborn baby may have all of these. After the embryo has grown past the stage of being a fetus and has become a person, the sanctity of human life should be respected. I am among those who regard the unwanted, unpromising embryo as having no greater value than unjoined sperm and egg cells, which are also alive and human. I may be wrong.

Question: Do you really think that population growth can be stopped without the use of coercive methods?

Answer: I hope so. It is better to try to get cooperation by offering some sort of reward than to use methods that are forcible and rob people of freedom of choice. It seems probable that a dictatorship would be required to enforce coercive methods. As far as I am concerned, there is already far too much bureaucratic interference with human freedoms.

Question: It is claimed that as long as the final decision on bearing children is left to each individual, only the better educated with a social conscience will cooperate. Those who do not mind adding to social problems will outbreed those who care about man's future. Are you concerned about this possibility?

Answer: I am deeply concerned about it. I hope that offering material rewards to those not qualified to parenthood will be an effective way of getting their cooperation.

Question: It has been proposed that people of the middle and upper classes remain childless and adopt babies born to the underprivileged and that we should forget about encouraging the underprivileged to practice birth control. What do you think of this proposal?

Answer: I think that it is high foolishness. I have seen stickers in windows of houses and cars proposing this. The adoption of orphans by families who can offer a good environment is humane and useful. But why should any woman choose to bear a child just to offer it for adoption? If the reproduction load is born by welfare mothers there will be a steady decline in national competence.

Question: Why haven't you said more about predictions that it will soon be possible to repair and replace defective genes and to cure people who are born with genetic defects?

Answer: I don't think that such predictions will come true for several, perhaps many, decades.

Question: Have you anything more to say about predictions that egg cells can be fertilized outside the human body and grown into babies in artificial wombs?

Answer: This may become possible sometime but not soon. The natural way of having babies works very well, and there are plenty of men and women who are capable of being good parents to all the children the world needs. Many women would welcome freedom from childbearing, but if it does become possible to grow babies outside the human body, these procedures will have to be tested a long time before they are proven safe and in all respects desirable.

Question: Why are you opposed to a rigorous program of positive eugenics?

Answer: Because most of the experts in human genetics are opposed to it. It is true that the extensive use of artificial insemination by sperm taken from gifted men would be the most rapid way of increasing the intelligence of children. But medical science has too little knowledge of the risks involved in trying to breed a superrace. I have mentioned that animals bred selectively for some quality have sometimes developed undesirable traits as well. Racing animals are likely to be of nervous temperament. Some strains of purebred animals are overly aggressive and others are stupid and lazy. Some are abnormally sensitive to certain diseases. Although it may become possible to avoid these problems in man, it seems risky now. Another important reason for forgetting about breeding a superrace is that the average human being is capable of living a long happy life with reasonably good health, of doing his share of work at a needed job, and of being a good parent.

Question: Aren't you being inconsistent in claiming that you want human freedoms to be increased and then arguing that some people should be denied the right to have children?

Answer: No. Overpopulation causes extensive loss of

individual freedoms. The child who is enslaved by poor biological inheritance and by poor cultural inheritance has limited freedoms. I am willing to trade the freedom of adults to reproduce irresponsibly for greater freedoms for children.

Question: I need genetic counseling, but I can't find a counselor. What can I do?

Answer: If your family physician is not able to advise you, ask him to find a physician who has some training in this field. During the past ten or fifteen years a number of medical schools have offered courses in medical genetics. You are more likely to find a young physician with this training than to find an elderly doctor who knows how to advise you. A list of genetic counseling centers may be obtained from the National Foundation, Box 2000, White Plains, New York, 10602.

Question: What is medical science doing about prolonging life, and if it succeeds, how is this going to affect welfare and population problems?

Answer: My answers are oversimplified. People die of accidents and disease, and they die because of aging. Life expectancy has increased because a number of the great killing diseases can either be prevented or successfully treated. Further progress of this sort may be expected, but medical science has done nothing to slow down the aging process. In studies on laboratory animals it has been possible to prolong life in some species by restricting the intake of food. It is known that heredity is important in determining length of life in both animals and man. There are a number of different theories on the causes of aging, but no theory has been proven. Some biologists believe that the aging process is coded into our genes just as is the growth process. They think that it will become possible to change the genes of man so that he can live much longer. Some science writers and even some scientists predict that life span can be doubled, and a few imagine that a life span of a thousand years will become possible. I don't take such predictions seriously. I know most of the work going on in this field, and it doesn't seem to me that medical science is anywhere near being able to delay aging. The increase in average life span of even ten to twenty years would greatly increase the population and would increase the welfare problems unless man could be kept vigorous and able to work for longer times. Longer periods of senility are not desirable.

Question: Can you state any ethical principle that gives society the right to restrict the reproduction of some individuals while encouraging the reproduction of others?

Answer: I accept the principle that society has the right to restrict individuals from causing harm to other individuals and society. I believe in the right of society to exercise intelligent humane control over its future rather than to submit passively to irresponsible threats to its welfare and dignity.

Question: Isn't it going to become possible to turn most of man's work over to automated machines controlled by computers, thereby freeing most people from any need to work or seek careers?

Answer: I doubt that the further development of automation and computer control is going to free mankind from working or from responsibilities to society. I doubt that these developments will make everybody rich with all wanted goods available for the asking. It does mean that the jobs of the future will require more special training and planning. Simple manual jobs and simple clerical jobs are already disappearing. People of low intelligence and drives won't have a chance to exist except on welfare.

Question: Can't we solve the problems of overpopulation by colonization of other planets and the solar systems of other stars?

Answer: No. None of the other planets in our solar system will support life, and all other stars are too far away to reach in a reasonable time unless it becomes possible to travel much faster than light.

Question: I don't agree that any couples should be encouraged to have more than two children. Our social ills will grow horrendously if population growth is not checked. The threat of reproduction by those whom you judge to be unqualified for parenthood is much less than the danger of overpopulation.

Answer: I agree with your judgment on the threat of overpopulation, but if it becomes possible to control population growth it should be possible to do it selectively. If no couple has more than two children, the population of our country will eventually decrease. Some women do not mate. Some who mate are sterile. Some children die before they become parents. There are many millions of individuals who are poorly qualified for parenthood. If as many as half of them remain childless, then millions of couples who are highly qualified for parenthood could have three or more children without causing population growth.

Question: How does your aim to produce a more competent human race differ from that of Hitler's? Not the means by which it is brought about but the difference, if any, in underlying principle?

Answer: You used a key word "race" in your question. Hitler aimed to develop a "superrace of Aryans." By this he meant "Caucasians of non-Jewish descent." I do not judge qualifications for parenthood according to race, religion, or any group or class. Qualifications for parenthood should be judged solely in terms of individuality. Hitler engineered the deaths of millions of citizens of his country and started the greatest war in history to achieve his aims. His aims and methods were as unscientific as they were evil. They were the opposite of scientific humane means of working for the prevention of human misery.

Question: Suppose that voluntary control of population growth doesn't work. Would you then advocate government control over reproduction?

Answer: Having to make this choice would be like having to choose between having cancer or leprosy. I would probably cop out of making the choice and look for a hiding place.

Question: We have a citizen draft used for wars that involve much less than national survival. Why can't democracy recognize that overpopulation is a greater enemy and take whatever measures are needed to control it?

Answer: You have a good point, but one wrong cannot be used to justify another wrong. I regard the forcing of unwilling citizens to fight in unnecessary wars as an evil. I do believe that extraordinary powers over the individuals are necessary when defensive wars must be fought, and perhaps such powers will be necessary to control the population crisis.

Question: I like the idea of cloning, for it would be a means of making everyone biologically equal.

Answer: I regard biological diversity as more desirable.

Question: Why would anyone want to clone several Einsteins? Each would just rediscover the same things.

Answer: I suggest that you reread what I have said about the importance of environment in the development of the individual. Genetic identity does not produce biological and psychological identity, only some degree of similarity. Differences in experiences always occur and cause genetically identical individuals—one-egg twins—to differ in personality and achievement.

Question: Are you on the side of social control or on the side of free enterprise?

Answer: I have a strong preference for freedoms over anything more than voluntary controls. Freedoms are possible when linked with the voluntary assumption of responsibilities. Many people abuse their freedoms and fail to assume responsibilities. They interfere with the rights and freedoms of others so that social controls become necessary. I could write for a long time about the misuse of both freedoms and controls without giving any new ideas as to what our socio-economic system should be like. I do think that society should do pilot experiments on proposed changes and should study carefully the experiences of other societies rather than to work by trial and error.

Question: Do you think that our society is likely to adopt selective population control?

Answer: The odds are against it.

XIV

Summary

The principal points made in this book are the following:

1. Society must control population growth.

2. Parenthood is not an inherent right; individuals differ in their qualifications for parenthood.

3. Parenthood is not an obligation; no woman should be required to bear an unwanted child.

4. Some couples should remain childless because of the high risk that their children would inherit biological bases of poor health and incompetence.

5. Some couples should remain childless because they cannot offer children the sort of environment needed for good health, citizenship, and self-sufficiency.

6. Every child should have the right to a sound biological endowment and good environment, including a sound cultural endowment.

7. Couples who are highly qualified for parenthood may be encouraged to have larger-than-average families.

8. Efforts to create a good environment that includes equal rights and opportunities should continue.

9. Moral guides to selective population control should be encouraged by education and material rewards rather than by coercion.

10. Programs of selective population control should be in the hands of the medical profession and a new professional class of social scientists trained to judge qualifications for parenthood. The evolvement of programs should be guided by the outcomes of experiments with small pilot studies.

Suggested Readings

BEADLE, GEORGE AND MURIEL. *The Language of Life.*
Doubleday-Anchor, Garden City, New York, 1967.
This introduction to the science of genetics is writ-
ten for beginners by George W. Beadle, who won a
Nobel Prize for his research in genetics, and by his
wife, a gifted writer.

BETTELHEIM, BRUNO. *The Children of the Dream.* Mac-
millan, New York, 1969.
A humanistic description of the kibbutz in Israel
and the outcomes of this form of child training. The
author is a leading psychologist.

HARDIN, GARRETT. *Birth Control.* Bobbs-Merrill/Pegasus,
Indianapolis, 1970. BSCS Science and Society Book.
A guide to methods of birth control. It is lucid, care-
fully detailed, and illustrated.

KELLER, DOLORES E. *Sex and the Single Cell.* Bobbs-Mer-
rill/Pegasus, Indianapolis, 1972. BSCS Science and Society Book.
A well-written, nonsensuous account of sex with
particular reference to its cellular basis.

KLEMM, WILLIAM C. *Science, the Brain and Our Future*. Bobbs-Merrill/Pegasus, Indianapolis, 1972. A BSCS Science and Society Book.

     An intriguing account of some of the latest knowledge about the brain and its role in human behavior.

LeBARON, RUTHANN. *Hormones: A Delicate Balance*. Bobbs-Merrill/Pegasus, Indianapolis, 1972. A BSCS Topics in Biology Book.

     The author clearly and concisely reviews the functions and interactions of the various hormones. There are some errors on the history of hormone research.

MARK, V. H. AND F. R. ERVIN. *Violence and the Brain*. Harper and Row, New York, 1970.

     The authors review the relationship of the brain to violence and show that at least some people are likely to become violent because of brain disease.

McKUSICK, VICTOR A. *Human Genetics*. Prentice-Hall, Englewood Cliffs, New Jersey, second edition, 1969.

     Written for biologists and physicians by a leader in the field of human genetics. It is clearly written, but some background information is needed by the reader.

VOLPE, E. PETER. *Human Heredity and Birth Defects*. Bobbs-Merrill/Pegasus, Indianapolis, 1971. A BSCS Science and Society Book.

     This clearly written, well-illustrated book describes the known causes of birth defects and the available methods of predicting and detecting them.

WILLIAMS, ROGER J. *You Are Extraordinary*. Random House, New York, 1967.

     The author is a distinguished biochemist in the fields of nutrition and biology. The book describes individual differences among people.